MAKING
MANIFEST

MAKING
MANIFEST

On *Faith*, *Creativity*, and the *Kingdom* at Hand

DAVE HARRITY

 seedbed

Cover design by Stephanie Wright

Page design by PerfecType, Nashville, TN

Library of Congress Control Number: 2013931139

Paperback ISBN: 978-1-62171-008-0

Printed in the United States of America

13   14   15   16   17   6   5   4   3   2   1

SEEDBED PUBLISHING
Sowing for a Great Awakening
204 N. Lexington Avenue, Wilmore, Kentucky 40390
www.seedbed.com

For Rod and Jae—

your words matter.

contents

Week 3

Week 4

acknowledgments

This book would not be possible if it weren't for several dedicated individuals who—by their contributions of provoking discussion, careful reading, and generous offerings of time and kindness—pushed me to finish; I'd like to acknowledge a few here. To the folks at Seedbed and Asbury Seminary for their creativity, care, and attention to detail. To my students, whose voices and discussions were the seeds for this book. To Karen McDavid, Rod Dixon, Michael Winters, Paul Quenon, Jae Newman, John David Walt, Dan Bowman, and Callid Keefe-Perry for their suggestions and work on this book, and to the writers, teachers, and scholars I admire, who took their time to read and endorse the book—your words mean so very much. And, a special thank-you to Drew Causey, who worked diligently to makes suggestions and anchor me in the ideas that this book needed—this would be a lesser book without you. And, lastly, to my family—none of this is possible without your love, inspiration, and support, especially Amanda and our children, who live with me even when it's tough. And to my parents, who set me on this path long ago.

Several parts of this book appeared in other publications before appearing here, and I'd like to acknowledge those people and magazines. Thank you to Bobbi Buchannan at *New Southerner* for publishing "Your Days Are Waiting"; to Laura Barkat at *Tweetspeak* for allowing me to reflect in "Coming to Poetry"; to Tania Runyan and Brad Fruhauff at *Relief Journal* for publishing "Ghost Story"; and to the fabulous Brianna Van Dyke for her support and belief in my work from the beginning, and for publishing "To Mark the Place," parts of "The Whole World," and "Works with Soul Interview" (conducted by Keira Havens) in *Ruminate Magazine*.

to begin

1. using this book

This 28-day devotional book is grounded in the acts of writing, creativity, imagination, solitude, and community-building, all designed to help you "re-vision" the way you understand and interact with the Kingdom of God. For the next month, let this book replace your devotional activities and routine, and allow the practices of daily writing and reflection to be born or more fully embodied as you spend time working through this text by yourself and/or with others.

Each day contains one meditation and one writing exercise—activities totaling about a half hour. The meditations are short, thought-provoking points of contemplation—sometimes accessible, sometimes obscure. Here's what they aren't: puzzles that need to be solved or riddles designed to stress you out. They're meant to incline your heart and mind toward mystery, wandering, seeking, exploring, and contemplating. If you're unsure about this, wouldn't call yourself creative, need more convincing, or desire a little guidance on how to cultivate an imaginative, creative and/or devotional life, flip to the back of the book and take a look at the "Five Practices for Believing Writers," which will give you some pointers on how to get the process started. It's my belief that ALL people can be creative since the act of creating is something we're designed to *do*—maybe you simply need to expand your definition of the word *creative*. This book will help you do that if you make it part of your daily life.

Each meditation ends with a writing exercise of some kind—a call to journal, describe, reflect. Use the lines provided in this book to complete the assignments, or use your own journal, notebook, paper—whatever is simple, convenient, coherent—if you'd like more room. Either way—whatever you choose to do—be sure to complete the activities in a space that's your own, where you can take risks, be boldly honest, and open yourself to the process over the product.

Take heart in knowing that you're not writing for quality like you might in a class-room; you're writing to bring forward the truth living in you in all its complex variety. It's simply putting down words, not much more—a little bit of intentional scribbling, creative thinking, an awareness of the world around you. You shouldn't worry or panic about having to write. Simply do your best work—be slow and purposeful, knowing that the truest meaning of what you're creating is already realized: it's present and whole as it stands before you. Can it be made better? Sure, but don't worry about that while you're writing. At the end of each week, as a final exercise, you'll compile your scribblings into the beginnings of a poem. Again, quality isn't as important as effort. If you take a step of faith forward, your words will rise to meet and guide you. That sentence will make more sense later, as you take those steps of faith.

Keep in mind, this is not so much a devotional book as a series of daily engagements oriented toward quiet action. I say this because this book is intended to help you *make* something, *build* something, *create* something. The meditations are a slow cooker for your spiritual growth, ruminations that seek to guide you to an imaginative path where cultivating your Christian life and discipline is valuable because it's creative as well as pragmatic.

What's more, this book is designed to be used in the quiet space of your own home, during your devotional practice, but can also be used communally in corporate worship, study, and practice. In the back of this book, you'll find a "Community Building" section with a handful of resources, including group writing exercises, discussion questions, revision pointers, and other sundries to aid you and your faith community in the seriously fun effort of bringing faith and imagination together— entering a sacred space where these forces can collide. I hope this will grow to be a unique resource—an innovative movement of awakening for believing communities.

As for coming together weekly as a community over the month of working with this book, there are three distinct activities people can participate in together:

- *Group Discussion*: The back of the book contains discussion questions on each of the book's four sections and the poems around which each section is anchored. The questions are reflective, often asking for personal reactions, but also cover ideas about poetry, faith, and writing.
- *Writing Exercises*: There are four large group writing exercises, one for each meeting of your group over the twenty-eight days. Each one requires about thirty minutes to be completed. Of course, you can do these exercises solo if you're doing the book on your own. Consider them four bonus cuts!

- *Workshop*: This activity asks participants to *share their writing* from over the course of the week. This is overwhelming for some, but the shy among you should be comforted by the fact they're wandering the wilderness together, and that sharing writing—which in this case is distinctly personal—is a great way to build community, and quickly. It necessitates vulnerability right from the start.

Clearly, unless groups are meeting for a long amount of time—about two and a half hours—they will not be able to get to all three of these activities in a single session. It's my suggestion that two activities are tackled within an hour to an hour-and-thirty-minute span. That way, the group can move slowly through the material and really listen, engage, and support one another. Of course, if you'd like to meet longer, you should do so!

The ultimate aim of this book is two-fold: first, to demystify writing practice, but not domesticate it; second, to give you and your faith community the tools you'll need to create art, live intentionally in and outside your own religious community, and explore the mysteries of your faith through acts of writing, like journaling and poetry. It's been my experience that creative groups of people form robust and lasting connections, and it's my hope that that effect might translate to our faith communities as well. We have the chance, as believers, to grow together in unwavering awareness of the reality of our belief by way of our imaginations. Wisdom, faith, and peace are all acts that reach their fullest potential in community, and, as Christians, we'll need those ingredients to rouse and realize the Kingdom of God within and around us.

2. what should happen

Writing is intimidating at first, so it would be good for you to pause and breathe before you begin—don't be rattled or racked. Your words may not be pretty or perfect—especially at first—but they will be real: little imaginative creations, small works of *your* hand, manifestations of God's Spirit in you. So don't worry about quality as much as completion—just move through the book and let things happen—run the race, pace yourself. No pressure. If you're still fretting, be comforted by the idea of revision—where everything is possible and anything can change—which is briefly discussed at the end of the book. So often we think of writing as fixed, when in reality it's a living process. Remember, you only see writing—typically—in its finished, published form. But there was a road that led to publication that's littered with trash, junk, lovely distractions, and brilliant observations that just didn't quite fit. You'll certainly be making some of those things as well.

For those of you who aren't particularly interested in writing poems, but are interested in writing of other kinds—like journaling, fiction, or creative non-fiction—know that the practices learned in this book will carry over nicely to your other creative projects and practices. If you want to cultivate your skills as a writer, poetry is the place to start since it utilizes all the skills you'll need to write with confidence and enthusiasm: attention to words—both in diction and sonic value; evocative construction of those words into images and metaphors cast over lines; narrative pace and tension; and brevity, which will help you craft vivid and readable prose, as well as help you learn what should be kept in and what should be left out, since what is not said is often as important as what is, and vice-versa. Learning to write poetry will help you in all other kinds of writing (and even art-making) since poetry and narrative share the same DNA—their highest aims exactness, tightness, and fluidity—using language to craft a coherent picture of being a human in the world. We'll be working toward that high ambition.

If you're a Christian and an attentive reader of Scripture, then poetry's value should be inherently clear: much of Scripture is written as poetry. Furthermore, Christianity's contributions to the development of English poetry are rich, varied, and invaluable—helping to shape the craft and complexity of the art form. So know that you're taking your place in these traditions—it's time for you to make a contribution, even if it's just a small one.

Every day, all you'll need is a pen or pencil and this book. There's space for you to write, but of course, if you'd rather work in a journal of your own, go right ahead. Mull over the Scripture selections and think of their connections—direct or indirect—to the meditations and exercises. Scribble, question, reflect, revive—be aimless and wander with your words. No boundaries, grades, or judgments. And be sure this book is well-worn by the time you're done—crack the spine so the book rests flat, dog-ear, sketch and scratch—abuse it. No journal is complete until there's at least one coffee ring or tea stain on one of the pages.

Lastly, a word of advice: as you work here, try to live here too. Make this activity the touchstone of your day—the activity out of which you live each moment. Work hard enough in this book that you leave the world for a bit, but not so hard that you remove yourself from the world completely. Devotional practices are for orientation toward loving the world, not escaping it. They should bring our reality into a focused vision, whereby our newly sharpened sight—our revitalized senses—can help us see the world more as God sees it. This book is not easy, but don't stop working through it. Do it with a friend or group and pace one another, push through days where you don't feel like writing. Be sure to complete the program, even if you can only do a little work each day. The reflections and exercises build on one another so that you can track the small but powerful changes happening in your life and words. I know it's tough to make it happen, but you'll be rewarded for your efforts—you'll make things you would have never made otherwise.

Move through these pieces—poems, reflections, Scriptures, and exercises—day by day, and expect something to change in you. Not because of anything that's been written in the pages by me, but because you're taking time to allow for quiet and creativity in a way that you hadn't before. Writing—much like the Kingdom of God—is a place where nothing is ever wasted, where all time spent is good time. The Kingdom Way of being isn't focused on how we think so much as the small rightnesses we realize because they've existed in and around us all along. So let's move forward together and more fully enter the deep world of words.

MAKING
MANIFEST

Now go and write down these words.

Write them in a book.

They will stand until the end of time as a witness.

—Isaiah 30:8 NLT

{ 1 }

Your Days Are Waiting

There's a sound like certainty a river makes,
the steady way leaves float the surface like paper
    boats.
Or the noise of hooves throbbing in purple light.
There's a waking in every wilderness.

What is inside your mind
that waits to slip away?

Will you remember what it was like to stare
into the constant face of the moon? To watch
the jet stream's hand push clouds through night?
And stars like ships on the ocean?

Your days are waiting to be left behind.
So now, before sleep or waking make you forget,
etch in yourself
this moon,
this leaf,
this star.

1 | enter here

For we are God's poemia, <u>created</u> in Jesus Christ to do good works,
which God prepared in advance for us to do.

—EPHESIANS 2:10

Picking up this little book means something. Picking it up each day will mean something greater. For the foreseeable future, you have an opportunity to awaken and engage your spirit in a way you may never have before: through creative and journal writing, by the natural poetry and story of your life.

Here you are, reading—this moment of your existence flashed onto the reel of your life forever. It might be something you forget—the reel placed in a canister and shelved. Or it might be something you replay over and over in your mind—the reel flickering meaning, reviving something that opened your eyes. That moment may or may not be today. It may or may not be tomorrow.

You've chosen this—what you're doing is intentional. You could be doing something else right now: cooking, watching a movie, riding a bike, working, running errands— and maybe you'll do those things today—but right now you are doing *this*.

Even in this moment there's a space inside you opening, however slowly. All the things you've taken in recently through your senses are simmering in you. How will those things roll to a boil?

Even in this moment you're turning your attention to something different. Think of how far these words had to travel to find you. It's a miracle you're reading them at all. Now, they're occupying your attention, at least that's the hope. Can you fathom the chances?

And even now a space is being made in you for what hasn't happened yet, a space for your life and experience to come: you'll internalize what's being read here and it will mix with the other ingredients of your days, and those things will commune with each other, live together, fashion, modify, and redefine some new idea—open the eyes of some dormant animal asleep inside your mind.

Here's something lovely: out of that space, who you are emerges. You—your life—as a work of art, some way forward to a new voice. So these things—these moments you thought were small—aren't really so small after all: they are the entirety of you. Already in you is God's living, creating Spirit, a *poemia*—a workmanship—waiting to transpire.

Mystical, I know. But this is a mystical book in a way—a platform off which you might jump into the magnificent obscurity of who you are and who you are becoming, and jump daily. An unknown place that will lead you into the very heart of God.

God is making and remaking, creating and revising—in creation, through Incarnation, and into new creation; God is reimagining the whole of this created world. The heart of God began beating in the Incarnation and has pulsed in the world since Creation. The Incarnation: *Word* made *Flesh*. God has come; Language has skin. Construction is the ultimate result of our words. Christ, then, is God's ultimate poem, God's ultimate workmanship—*poemia* in Greek, which is where we also get the English word *poem*. Poetry is the richest use of our human language: carefully crafted words rendering powerful experience, telling the story of human condition. Our words, designed—fleshed out.

And our words come from inside. When God spoke creation was born, Christ was born, and you were born. The words of creation are born in you—every moment since, and in the moment of now. That *poemia* is our birthright, and we're brought into that refinement by the grace of Christ's body.

So our language isn't just for communicating—it's for co-creating, it's for communing. With our words, we bring realities into being, we track our history, we polish our present, and we carve out the direction of our future; we renew, awaken, and build toward redemption.

Our words are the place where we begin. ༄

{ exercise 1 }

Re-read the poem that begins this week's series of meditations. Take some time to think about the way you see the world—what's it like to live with your uniqueness? It's something we don't often think about. Your hairs are numbered and your being known. So, tell about it. Give some serious thought to what it's like being you.

Are you a glass-half-full or half-empty person? A black-and-white or gray person? Are there times when you see only what you want? Or do you consider yourself a diplomat—seeing the world from many angles? Why? Or are you something different all together?

What do you want to see in the world? What do you hope for? What people and events have shaped your vision? What informs it most? Dig deep.

What is it that you want to *say* to the world? What do you want your voice to be *for*?

2 | life as a poem

Be still before the Lord
and wait patiently for him . . .

—Psalm 37:7

When God reveals, it's in a voice of poetry. Even without the Psalms and the Prophets, the language of Scripture is overwhelmingly cast as poetry—intentional, careful, vibrant language. It's the language God uses to raise our eyes and incline our hearts—draw us into an abiding vision of what's been created, of the ever-important—and disappearing—instant.

Awake and see.

Words for reverence and response.

Calling.

We aren't God for many reasons, but maybe most of all because we aren't nearly as precise with our words, or as creative. We spend most of our lives trapped between saying too much and not saying enough, and in both cases we rarely come close to saying something completely. We're always using our language to try and say what can never be fully said. Most of our life is ineffable. Yet we're using words everywhere—in our media, in our literature, in our music, and in our conversations. Do we make these noises with our words because we fear the quiet that comes forward when noise fades?

Those quiet moments often scare us. Maybe we feel we wouldn't know what to say or how to articulate the way an encounter with quiet makes us feel; maybe we don't like the way quiet makes us feel. We're lost between experience and the way we render that experience or reconcile it back to who we are—we're all lost in translation. We haven't quite arrived at that unshakable contentment, but are quite aware of its presence. We're already seeing, but not yet envisioning.

To do all of this—to come close to saying what can't be said or being what we can't fully be—we have to choose to set aside time to meet this becoming, to respond to God's incarnate invitation of full awareness. **We need *solitude* in a world that wants to visit, *quiet* from a world that wants idle chit-chat, and *steadfastness* in a world where everything's changing and transient.** We need time to gather the little pieces of ourselves that scatter. We need time to write down our little lives.

The good news: your life is already *poemia*—a living, breathing work of words. So with a little time and practice each day, your bit of energy will become worship you make, not worship made for you. Will you be the greatest writer to walk the earth? No. Will you even be one of the best? Probably not. But those labels are subjective, fallacious, junk: you simply should want to be your voice—honest and real regardless of what the world might think. You can best worship God by accepting your words and giving them life, by owning them, and then giving them back; or, as Romans 12:1 says, to present them as part of your reasonable sacrifice—offering your words as part of offering yourself.

So expect all things to change when you start to write—your habits, your ideas of the world, the song you sing silently to yourself each day. An alertness will materialize from seeking; some great smallness will come. That's what will happen when you embrace *this moment*, make it manifest in ink and paper, pencil and page. ∾

{ exercise 2 }

Choose three words from the list of twenty-four below—circle them. What you're about to do might be a challenge, but it's worth some serious effort. Go ahead and choose . . .

break	weave	fire	temper
braid	lilt	cairn	ditch
crave	left	bruise	patch
bilk	gravity	blame	clarity
track	bind	callous	smoke
home	bury	blaze	crutch

Now define those words, but not as you would see them in the dictionary—you should use your experiences. Think of an event from your memory (often childhood is a most fruitful avenue) to go along with each of your choices. These words—the ones you chose—are anchored in your subconscious. Time to do some divining.

_____

_____

_____

_____

_____

It helps if you take a minute to repeat each word quietly to yourself. Close your eyes and say each word ten times over. When you open your eyes, what image emerges in your mind? That's how you're defining the word down deep—where does that definition come from? Tell about it.

_____

_____

_____

_____

_____

_____

Write out a few sentences for each of your three choices—tell the stories and definitions behind these words with brevity, tersely. Don't worry if it makes sense or seems strange. We're going for truth—not beauty—right now. It's okay if none of this makes a bit of sense. It will flesh itself out later.

_____

_____

_____

_____

_____

3 | here i am

Now Moses was tending the flock . . . and he led the flock to the far side
of the wilderness and came to Horeb, the mountain of God. There the angel
of the Lord appeared to him in flames of fire from within a bush. Moses saw
that though the bush was on fire it did not burn up. So Moses thought,
"I will go over and see this strange sight—why the bush does not burn up."

When the Lord saw that he had gone over to look, God called to him from
within the bush, "Moses! Moses!"

And Moses said, "Here I am."

—Exodus 3:1–4

You are here. In this place.

You chose it. Or maybe it has chosen you. Or maybe you were chosen for it. Any is all right. Your life right now—no matter what—is what it's supposed to be.

Do you believe that's possible?

Think of all the things that emerged in your experience that led you to this room—all the love and tragedy you've lived. Gain and loss. Peace and chaos. All of it so real and present here.

Think of all the people that once occupied this space, their lives. Lives you'll never fully know or understand. Each of us has our own secrets. Even you.

And those people and their lives were just as real and unknown as you: rustling, wrestling, communing, complaining, crashing, creating. Where are they now? Do they remember the place you are right now? Is it a brightness in their mind or a fading away? You'll never know the prominence of this place.

You're part of a history that you can never know.

You're living a present that you can't fully comprehend.

You're making a future that can't be controlled.

So don't hinder this moment with worry or obtuse frustration since it—as you read this—is arriving as a gift beyond what you can fully wrap your head around. You breathe again. Another moment. All of it a careful orchestration. It just might be the New Heaven and New Earth.

Some people put providence away, pack destiny into a box. They call these mystical allowances in our lives idealistic, archaic, and naïve. They grow cynical toward faith. And maybe they're right. Certainly this world has its illusions, some of which modulate to delusions. But is that what's going on here? Are we deceiving ourselves with every passing second? Are we deceiving ourselves right now?

It's possible, and we're fools if we don't admit it. But what if all the off-ended notes, sidetracks, bursts, blares, punches, and flares are all building some wild and authentic architecture? What if each cut in the earth were a river rolling to some vast sea? What if these passages of time accumulating in you are boomeranging back to the hand of this very instant?

What if all those flashing moments of time lead right up to the question mark that ends this sentence?

The hard truth for the cynics: that's a possibility as well. Possibility is what we're made of—always on the cusp of beginning and completion, always opening and closing.

And here we pick up the purpose of an author, a seeker, a creator. We're walking on a wire across the cavernous gap of two summits: calculation and chaos. Your life inhabits both sides at once in a delicate balancing act—your propensity to thrive between peaks of knowing and unknowing. Maybe we should spend some time in this suspended space.

What has come before you in this place? What objects might have filled this room? Do those essences still linger? How many people have seen the moon from that window? Watched light cut away shadows at dawn? Can you smell what used to live or be here? Can you remember what this room first looked like when you arrived? Or has your presence changed it so completely that it's shaped your memory?

Imagine the face of Moses—breathless in shock to learn the truth and say it back. "Here I am" meaning something more like *behold me, take me, choose me*. I am before you. I am the offering. This is my moment. And I will live it as a gift.

This ground is holy. God is with us. The history of the present is burning all around you. You may live here now, but that will change and some new person will come and be here. And they'll be unaware of this moment—your presence—and what you've made in this place. Like trees losing leaves in autumn, everything will change beyond you. Again and again.

Maybe you'll be that new person when you return here later today.

We live in the space of the possible, not just the actual. Some of us just acknowledge the possible—choose to see it, abide it, embrace it, name its shape in stars. Maybe those of us who do are poets—individuals who seek to know the world, to be in the world, to love the world enough to bear witness to it, to offer ourselves for its sake. We're living *here*. *Here* we are.

We must take the certainty of uncertainty and render it into words, make it into a way for remembering. Open your eyes to the possible here: you are alive in the world; this is your life. And you've made it this far. You and I are the guest who's always arriving. The story that's beginning again each day. Write that experience in *your* words. You must begin to listen.

Blank pages listen. Always. They never fight back. They don't judge. They won't turn you away. They won't give you a stone if you ask for bread. In fact, they're an invitation to notice what's possible, to notice what's complete. Pages aren't complete till our words arrive and make them perfect, useful, vibrant. Pages don't make mistakes.

Whatever you've been told in life matters little to the reality that in this second you're complete—you only have to awaken to it.

Here. Now. Here. Now. This moment. *This* moment.

This one too.

The world is waiting to be left behind *and* it's also rising to meet you. Before all the distractions of this place help you forget who you are, who you've been, who you want to become—write down what you can: your moon, your leaf, your star. ☙

{ exercise 3 }

1. What are the events that led you to this moment? Take a minute to think about some recent epiphanies in your life—some moments of awakening and realization. Moments of *poemia*. Pick one and reflect on it in no more than ten sentences (and no less!)

_____

_____

_____

_____

_____

_____

_____

_____

2. Describe what it's like to sit where you're sitting right now. Pay close attention. What do you sense? Describe your surroundings a bit by providing rich sensory descriptions—what do you see, hear, feel, smell, and taste? How are those senses affected by the time of day, your mood, your attention?

No detail is insignificant.

Again, have no worries about the beauty of what you're writing, just attention to the truth of it. Capture, clarify, claim. Again, ten sentences.

_____

_____

_____

_____

_____

_____

3. Answer this question in ten sentences: what does it feel like to be you in this moment?

_____

_____

_____

_____

_____

_____

_____

{ exercise 4 }

Before you read today's meditation, you're going to do some writing.

Tell about a time when you felt a vivid sense of awe—when you were speechless, frozen, or dumbstruck. Remember, dig deep. And don't necessarily go for the first thing that pops up. Retell the story below in your own words, doing justice to the moment's importance, immensity, and beauty by your words—details, honesty, reflective sensory descriptions.

Ok, go!

_____

_____

_____

_____

_____

_____

_____

_____

4 | one autumn

We were trick-or-treating and had gone out long before dusk so that we might make it back home reasonably close to the kids' bedtime. We paced the sidewalks with friends, knocked on doors, and watched as the children—for the first time—experienced the magic of masks, spooky homes, and free candy. They beamed in delight at the treats and trinkets—smiles and elation that can only come with being given a gift with no strings attached. Something like amazement, but more like awe.

The kids skipped, keeping pace through a lovely fall evening—the best fall we'd had in years. Door after door of strangers *oohhhing* and *awwwwing* at the pirate and fairy princess. The sunset distinctly autumnal—a silvery pink battered against the bare trees and their golden edges. Leaves blowing, vibrant reds and yellows; the air crisp with the bold smoke of chimneys. Everything was ringing right around the block, each family and their small celebration.

Before we knew it—the adults caught up in the fervor as well—the sun was almost gone and the kids were losing steam—sugar-stark, unwinding. The purple of the night was new to my kids who sleep long hours and are used to seeing the sun start to set and start to rise—light already splashing starlight away. We lost track of time, fully engrossed in our mutual exchanges of sweetness. The kids started dragging, and then it was actually dark; we'd made our way up and down the whole block back to the car. The circuit complete, we said goodbye to our friends. Our first Halloween a successful venture.

As I scooped up my son, now nearly deadweight from being so tuckered out, he said, "Daddy, I want bed now." Cute, of course. And he nuzzled my neck, sighing deeply. "I like trick-treat, Daddy . . ." he said. "I know you do, Bub. I like it too." And then he shot up, as if he suddenly noticed it was dark—and began squirming anxiously. He pulled himself back from me and craned his neck to see the path before us—soft street-lamps, slight shadows, dark images of people, distant laughs. "Daddy . . . I scared," he whispered. He started to shrink. "But look, Bub—look at the sky." I pointed up.

Those little light messages—miracles hanging over us. My boy breathed another sigh, but it was distinct with comfort, with awe. To the battery of little lights he said quietly, almost as a reflex, "Wwwwoooowwww . . ." and then stared speechlessly.

I think of the psalmists—the frail and unnamable fire of veneration, that one can only begin and end with questions about who we are together, who we will become: "When I consider your heavens, the work of your fingers, / the moon and the stars, which you have set in place, / what is mankind that you are mindful of them, / human beings that you care for them?" That's as close as I can come—the braided states of wonder, reverence, and amazement.

All of me awed—seeing this heavy world brand new. Or, in the case of my boy, for the first time. In the distance between us and the stars is the possibility of awakening—an invitation to see the mystery of living, and be glad in its infinity. The work of God's creation at large above us every night—almost like evidence that we are not alone or adrift, waiting at the doorstep of some empty house.

Me and my boy and our eyes pointed upward. Every night that comes close seems like one more proof of the phenomena we are, our holy bodies—and the honor of eyes that see. ∾

5 | kingdoms

The kingdom of heaven is like treasure hidden in a field.
When a man found it, he hid it again, and then in his joy went and sold
all he had and bought that field.

—Matthew 13:44

We're living vessels of God's presence in the world for mercy and love. Who you are in the world matters, and how you recognize the Kingdom of God within you brings Christ's hands into the immediate present.

While Christ's hands were here to hold ours long ago, we can't hold them physically here now, but the Spirit of the Incarnate God is everywhere, moving in and through us. And there are many ways to bring about that Kingdom in our world—acts of peace and charity, of course, seem the most obvious. A life of very real and very vivid grace—living faith.

But is there something we can do in *this* moment alone, while collecting thoughts, preparing? How about we do what God did to make all moments: *create*. Our God is one who imagines, makes, and revises. *See* our world, and *see* the being you are. And see Christ—an ultimate act of creation—God's being made real, dancing, walking, moving among the made.

And that's not an easy thing to wrap the mind around—it takes careful contemplation to approach a remote understanding of God being revised into something like us.

One of the saddest realities about life is that people have the choice whether or not to search for truth. While searching and seeking might be good and noble ways to live, they aren't necessary to living; you can go through all your days with your eyes completely open and never really see anything clearly. And one needs only to look around at the hollowness of the cultures around us, both secular and Christian, to know this can be true.

Christianity can be made simple, boiled down to practices and platitudes, marketed and packaged for sale, and fall flat with sentimental longing for some other plane of living rather than the reality in which God has asked us to exist—the reality that he loves so dearly.

But the Kingdom of God is nothing simplistic: realities like the Incarnation and Resurrection can never be made easy. That's mystery, and searching mystery is how we grow and bring forth that exquisite empire inside.

That's the funny thing about kingdoms: they never stay hidden for long. We become what we're ruled by. And we always adopt the economy of the kingdom living in us and introduce it to our world. Sometimes that economy is one of pain and isolation; other times it's of peace and community. Sometimes it moves between them.

Whether it's a kingdom of your own making or a kingdom that already occurred before you were awakened to its existence—what's in darkness is brought to light.

When you explore the Kingdom of God within through focused daily prayer, meditation, creating, or journaling, a quiet dominion emerges in you—a hamlet tucked away in a foggy mountainside: there's been life there all along.

Great, huh? Just one catch—you have to work a little. Not a graceless kind of guilty requirement that many pursue, but a slow and attentive way of being and moving forward—moving slowly instead of running; searching in prayer instead of insisting. It's a narrow and uneasy way—but that was the promise, right? To find the treasure you're going to have to turn over earth.

Is it possible we might sing in silence, that we might be complete in brokenness? Can we gain our lives by losing them or be made whole as we give away? You might not be strong enough to face all this day has to offer. And that's okay, because God is near to us; God has already come. Be remade in the world.

Christ himself is an invitation; he calls us to come into the world and create alongside God. Accept it by realizing what's already here now—the instruments necessary for making and remaking. Practice creation. Practice building. Practice being. And any habits that lead you to completing. Writing can be practiced like this, breathing worlds in and out; take the near-nothing before you and stir it into some unique beauty. Realize God in *this* world.

Words reflect both the Maker and the made. Maybe that's a way we can uncover the Kingdom. Sit quietly, pencil in hand; some small piece of it will come. Get out your small shovel and push it into the ground, smiling. ᑫ

{ exercise 5 }

Today, you're going to observe and scribble. Trust and follow—know that what might seem insignificant is actually helping you see more clearly.

Look at the objects around you. What's there that sticks out at you? Choose an object. Why do you think it sticks out? Can you describe it? Can you tell its story? Where does it come from? What's its significance to its owner? Why *that* object? Write ten sentences telling about it.

_____

_____

_____

_____

_____

_____

_____

_____

Now, describe what it's like to write the way you've been writing the past couple of days. Does it annoy or frustrate you? Rouse or exhilarate you? Why, do you think? Hypothesize. What do you think that writing like this each day might do to you emotionally, spiritually? How can it change your life?

6 | space & silence

*. . . being confident of this, that he who began a good work in you will carry it
on to completion until the day of Christ Jesus.*

—PHILIPPIANS 1:6

The Kingdom of God is breaking in—inside us and around us. We're becoming new creations, all our words and movements trekking toward this good work. As soon as we realize we've started, we've already begun and are closer to complete.

Christ is in the "arrived" of us and the "becoming" of us. This is completion—*poemia* taking hold. Air, light—elemental, apprehended. Before we begin to breathe in and make our words, we're opened to the slow, ever-emerging clarity that our spiritual condition is one of completeness—we arrive and ascend in the poetry of who we are.

Let's be clear: poetry begins you, though you might not know or feel it. You're alive in a world God made from words. And God's words have made you alive, and are making you more and more so.

It's funny to begin thinking of life as language, or language as an avenue to renewed life. Your life has always been and will always be the resting words of God—formed, animated, forward. God has been, is, and always will be present in our language, even when our language can only stutter toward freighted silence.

And that's the ache in us—silence. The silence of the page seen here:

a

The white space around the letter immaterial—the ink of the "a" dissipating the color of the page, carving itself out. This is what happens with our language every day. We fill our bodies and minds with similar noise—gather up the calamities of our days and try to shape them into something useful. Sometimes we can articulate our humanness. But our words will eventually fall short, like the print you're reading now. Even if we look at this page, even if we were to melt down all the ink and make it into a black block, that block could not come close to taking up a small fraction of space on the page—white silence radiating through, black brilliance stilled. Only when we let noise melt away can our truest voices emerge.

Colors aside, and despite the clamor of ink, the page is still the dominant force behind making the words. All of our words are defined by space and silence, the place and form in which they exist. Context is a revelation, a reckless grace bleeding through, a quiet and undeniable insurrection where we begin to awaken to the importance of this moment. Our words fix our lives to this space, this place, this time, this existence. None of us can survive without words.

When we sit—quiet and focused, still and silent—we embody awareness of space in and around us, the material of what's motionless—we pay attention and see the scope and shape of the world, where the horizon and plane become one expanse. And it can be disturbing or intimidating; in fact, it should be. The reality that we disturb something by living—something both physical *and* spiritual—is a hard reality.

Maybe it's our job to incline our hearts toward silence, to head for the slight grace that stillness allows from the noises of our world. Or maybe our job is to disrupt the silence just so, to make some arrival, some gentle voice, some concrete clarity, some step toward reconciling our presence.

Maybe peacemakers will be called children of God because they're attending to the world. Maybe the meek are blessed because they disturb so little. ∽

{ exercise 6 }

This one should get you thinking. Below, in Column A, is a list of common items found in a tool box. In Column B, you must make a list of items that you'd find in a kitchen—instruments, appliances, supplies, wares—anything, really. Here's the catch: the items listed in Column B must be close opposites of the items listed in Column A. It's strange, to be sure, but get creative here—use your imagination. Think about what the Column A objects represent on a deeper level—what they do, how they function. Grant yourself permission to be outlandish, to make mistakes, or say things that make little sense at first glance.

[column A]   [column B]

saw   _____

hammer   _____

pliers   _____

glue   _____

screwdriver   _____

ruler   _____

crowbar   _____

drill   _____

Now, reflect on your lists above. Select a few of your choices and explain your reasoning. Why are these things opposites? What are some patterns you see coming forward in this exercise? How do you think of objects? What do your choices tell you about the way your mind works, if you had to guess? Journal about it in the space below.

7 | being

Moses said to God, "Suppose I go to the Israelites and say to them,
'The God of your fathers has sent me to you,' and they ask me,
'What is his name?' Then what shall I tell them?"

God said to Moses, "I AM WHO I AM. This is what you are to say
to the Israelites: 'I AM has sent me to you.'"

—Exodus 3:13–14

Practices of words are practices of *being*—they stay with you when you walk away from this place, the place where you're reading this; they follow you to the next place where you'll have put away what's happening here to engage the immediate necessities of the moment. Words become touchstones for our thoughts, yardsticks for our growth. If you engage them, you begin to see how something like your "quiet time" or "devotions" can modulate into something like profound exploring, a wandering in the uncharted country of God's being—searching God's "I-AM-ness," searching for the face and heart of God.

Being is where we enter. Creating is an open door.

Yes, daily time reading Scripture and praying act as guards against the noise and chaos of the world, but is it possible that there's a little room for creation? Where do we take that noise and chaos and make something of it?

Writing is an active, but not busy, action—not business that impedes the contemplative or prayerful. It's a slowing way. And by that slowness, we invite God's presence into our walk. Maybe you already write a little—journal here and there, jot a poem or tell a story—which is wonderful practice. Could you see yourself doing it each day?

What might change if you did? Could you commit to a small shift that will result in a seismic reorientation toward poetry?

The critics, scholars, and smarties will want a definition, so here's an offering: Poetry is any act of intentional language that results in an act of creation, any act of making at all. But it isn't so much action as it is context. Because of the Incarnation, the poetry in us is complete, and we see our lives in light of that ultimate creation. When we aim our lives at the divine, we're beginning to become poetry. When we begin reflecting God's creativity by writing down our own words, we begin writing out the poem of our lives.

When you write as a creative spiritual practice—as a way of moving toward the divine—you begin to practice poetry, begin to notice poetry, and begin to realize *your* poetry.

Don't think too hard about it, since straight thinking rarely becomes an act of poetry—often times we think so hard about something that we destroy the poetry of it, which is the opposite of Incarnation: Annihilation. Sometimes we think a thing to death and our imagination atrophies. By poetry—just as by the Incarnation—we're invited into the divinity of the world, or maybe the divinity of the world opens itself to us.

Think of this sentence of prose:

> This morning when I rose from bed and looked at myself in the mirror, I came to accept that I'm like an image, not much more than a projection, but nothing less than right.

If we read those lines as prose, there isn't much to them—just a reflection on seeing oneself in the mirror. But if we break them into poetry then the mystery is exposed:

> This morning
> when I rose from bed
> and looked at myself
> in the mirror,
> I came to accept
> that I'm like an image,
> not much more

than a projection,
but nothing less
than right.

Not only do the lines control the flow of information—the lines are broken above to emphasize ideas within the poem and create an energy that moves us through the poem—but the lines create an anticipation absent in the prose version. The lines can be read alone to form their own contexts; the hidden phrases stand up straighter, closer to attention. Here, in the poem, we move and uncover each line, turning up a new stone and seeing the hidden world teeming underneath. What's above is poetry— maybe good, maybe bad—living and breathing. Quality matters less than authenticity at this stage.

This is what poetry makes in all of us: an allowance to live in the mysterious unknown, for edges to fray, for the pieces to fit in mosaic—it's permission for things to be messy. In poetry, we don't have to have the answers, or even fully know the questions. We don't have to get a ball over a goal line, climb a ladder, achieve, or do anything other than *be* and *experience.* Poetry is a way forward when we can't see which way to go. Poetry names what wasn't previously namable—makes the "I-AM-ness" clearer, allows us to sketch the outline of God with a little more clarity and accurate shadow.

Is it possible that our devotions and quiet times taper off or plateau, that without some act of creation we'll never move more fully into creation itself, into divine mystery? Maybe we should have trouble trusting people of faith who can't see the value in poetry, who don't like making with their words, or only use their words to convince others. Maybe we don't create because we're afraid that creation will make us move deeper into what's endlessly unknowable.

Maybe this white space

intimidates you. Maybe it should.

Because white space is always another beginning. And if we're facing a beginning, the rubble of an ending isn't far behind. The tension of the unknown is just in front of us. We become unsettled when spaces aren't filled for us. How can you name God—know the name of God—if your ears are closed, if you never drift into being by doing what God did, by creating?

Openings mean we must move into something unknown, that we must find a way forward, that we must pick up our mats and walk, that we must create something from thin air. And none of those things are ever easy. ❧

{ exercise 7 }

Go back through this week's notes and underline some stand-out phrases, ideas, introspections. Anything rising to attention? Calling out to you? Perhaps you've written something you feel proud of and don't know whether or not it's good. Who cares? If you think it's good, that's what matters now.

Try to weave together the ideas, even if they feel disparate. Remember, all of these words came from the same place: you. There's a connection, even if it's only slight. Try to add in a little something from each day you wrote this week—let your mind maneuver freely, associate without regard, and ask questions. Be comfortable with not knowing. Just try—knock and the door will be opened to you.

Write a ten-line poem that pays special attention to seeing something in a new light, recognizing something in a tiny but radical way. Tiny is a relative term here—get creative with it! It can be tiny in size, but also in significance: something very small or something that you pass each day and fail to notice. Just be sure that you're orienting yourself toward noticing and giving back what you see to the page. Title the poem "Awakening." Oh yeah, and no rhyming—don't you dare do it! Resist the urge. Because in these exercises you should be speaking organically, without trying to sound poetic. Let your voice shine through without the rhyming words that people so often associate with poetry.

Having trouble thinking of how to begin? Here's the first line:

I remember the way you used to speak to me,

_____

_____

{ 2 }

Ghost Story

You were thirteen when the carnival came to town.
A girl on the bus ride home from school, and you
    borrowed her favorite book—
ghost stories. She wrote her address in careful ink
    over the title page.

She lived close.
And that day you pedaled past her house. She never
    saw you,
never looked out because she was reading—her
    windows always paper, never glass.

At school, she asked to meet you there—
is there anything but yes?

The wheel stood high and bright over the ground,
    wrung calliope notes
between mechanical starts. You rode together again
    and again,
last autumn cool ribboning out over town, silver
    wave and mirrored twilight.

Stars set low; the bucket rocking itself.
The music sputtered and sank—the crowd moved
    below without affection.
She asked if you believed in ghosts.

What is it you said?
Your eye on the gleam of her hair—honey of her
    cheeks.
The way she said ghost made you want to believe.

Now it grows to shadow, doesn't it? Memory losing
    what it once held close—
how exactly does it end? What was her name?

As if you cupped your hands to drink—water leaking
    slow around the knuckles.

Her face is clear, smile freckled and shy.
The wheel clinking to revolve again.

But none of this matters: when you answered, she
    took your hand.

8 | with us

"For my thoughts are not your thoughts,
neither are your ways my ways,"
declares the LORD.

"As the heavens are higher than the earth,
so are my ways higher than your ways
and my thoughts than your thoughts . . ."

"You will go out in joy
and be led forth in peace;
the mountains and hills
will burst into song before you,
and all the trees of the field
will clap their hands."

—ISAIAH 55: 8–9, 12

There are few easy things about the way of Christ. And even though Christ says that his yoke is easy and his burden light (Matthew 11:30), those who follow him begin to wonder if this might be an oversimplification.

Especially since, before that, Christ—it would seem—goes to great lengths to convince us not to follow. Like in Matthew 10:37: "If you love your father or mother more than you love me, you are not worthy of being mine; or if you love your son or daughter more than me, you are not worthy of being mine." (NLT) Or Matthew 5:48: "Be perfect, therefore, as your heavenly Father is perfect." Or Matthew 10:34: "Do not suppose that I have come to bring peace to the earth. I did not come to bring peace, but a sword."

Yikes.

These words of Christ, cryptic and alarming, make Jesus a character *between* worlds—a world of comfort on one end and disturbance on the other. Often God's human coming seems a space of unsettling contradiction, especially when it comes to our desires for continuity, stability, and safety.

But when we can see that the contrasts are a reward and not a liability—that these contrasts can awaken and renew our faith in the power of the Incarnation—then we can begin to explore the richness of *God with us*. The language of God as human in Christ contributes something tremendous to our negative capability: the words of two worlds become one language—we're given new eyes to see the contradictions as contrasts, opposition as a different kind of attraction.

The Word made Flesh is the ultimate and unique moment of what language *can* become—the ultimate poetry of God—divinity walking upright, alive, bound up in creation. There it is again, that idea of workmanship. *Poemia* reimagines our potential so we might become a line in that poem.

So what does it mean to move forward toward what's complete, since Christ's *perfect*—as he said it—is more like *completeness* than flawlessness—a movement toward Isaiah's joy and peace. Certainly writing can lead to completeness—sensitizing us to the suffering and joy of the world, drawing us into the infinite, the two worlds of Christ's body and soul pushing us to move past our own lives. Our words, if we allow them, can be endless. And this is how they reflect our Maker.

We can be made toward God's completeness as we create, as we make with words. We're being formed, shaped, and revisioned by God's creating love. Writing is a way of reaching toward the void of the divine by making our own words flesh, but there's always something in us that hasn't quite arrived. We can reach as far as we'd like and still not hold the hand of God. This is what makes—or should make—the practice of being like Christ an unlimited pilgrimage. A journey always beginning and steps away from ending.

It's sad that we often forget that Christ and this world both began as acts of language. We boil down the teaching of Christ to clichés of right living, make the infinite mystery of God into a crass advertisement for something like placid salvation rather than radical redemption.

Since Christ is language, God's ultimate poetry has lived among us. The faith, hope, and love of Christianity cannot live where disciples pay little attention to words.

Christ's life isn't just an event in reality that saves us, but a whole and living word that compels us toward creation. Christ is that missing piece of the Maker to all of us—being and skin, words and hands. God came to earth—made from words—so that we might have a full life.

And people believe that what we say doesn't matter. What we say is often everything we are, revealed.

This should be a little intimidating, but any practice or effort that leads to fuller potential is, which is why we must move forward using our words. In the language of God that is Christ, there's a richness which one can begin to shape life around—a struggle against the self that drives us inward to a country of wilderness.

"Be *complete* as God is *complete*"—this is awakening to a life of intention, to engagement, to the poetry of our words. Here it is happening right now—and you can live it with or without intention. And it happens again and again—not tomorrow or next year, not on some metaphysical horizon or in some abstract afterness. Not with a promotion, or money, or meeting that person.

This.

Instant.

Right.

Now.

Here.

Awaken to it; incline your eyes toward the light glowing inside you. Here it is—the morning of who you are. Some dawn for your delight. Some small proof that you've been here, are being here, and will be here. That you made something *in* and *out* of this moment. That intentions are both desire *and* practice, clarity *and* life. How do you understand the pregnancy of this moment? How do you ask for change and know you're already complete? How do you ask the immanent language of God living in you to come closer?

You should open to these questions by closing your hands around a pen and writing it out.

Or maybe you're realizing that God is already near in the wild uniqueness of each second, that all that is is sacred. If only you could open your eyes to it. This *perfect* instant. This *perfect* place. ⌒

{ exercise 8 }

Re-read the poem that begins this week's series of meditations. What are some stand-out lines? What are some things that resonate? Give yourself time to think about this poem. What are some ideas that you find little value in? What isn't working?

_____

_____

_____

_____

_____

_____

Here's one: if you were writing a poem like this one, what might you leave *out*, and what might you add in? Your opinion matters.

_____

_____

_____

_____

_____

_____

_____

Here's one more: What do you think of the line breaks in this poem? Are they in the right place? Why or why not? Do any of them seem awkward to you? Or just right? Why do you think that is? And what about that title? What would you title this poem if you had written it?

Don't be shy—go ahead and tear into it! Write about it below.

_____

_____

_____

_____

_____

_____

_____

_____

9 | abide

I am the vine; you are the branches. If you remain in me and I in you,
you will bear much fruit; apart from me you can do nothing.

—John 15:5

Devotion is deep, but abiding is deeper.

When you're devoted to a cause, person, or purpose you act—you generate motion, make waves, push air and make it wind. This isn't bad—much of what is great about your life is built from devotion. But it can turn bad quickly. Devotion sours when it meets the wall where our abilities cease—where we just can't do it on our own. Devotion is the desert where we brush against frustration because our current capacity and energy have met some immovable mountain.

Devotion's exhaustion is exactly where abiding can begin to flourish. We begin by waiting patiently, void of expectation. Actions we often have trouble practicing. We like to think that everything is within our control—and some things are—but the reality is that showing up prepared for nothing is often the only thing in our control.

Will you continue writing when the act of it inevitably falls short of carrying you through? Not because you can't do it, but because—like many of the other things in your life that go unfinished—you're human and find your attentions being pulled toward something else?

Will you continue coming? Sticking out the road until the end of the path? Your choice.

This exchange of energy—the transfer from devotion to abiding—is reflected in the practices of writing: we wait for things to come to us by showing up faithfully each day. Some days things will be clear and come right away; other days you'll have to wait and wait, and even then only a little bit of something will come—and this might not hold against that high standard of worth you've placed on things that can never be measured right.

All other things will come forward if you do—you just need a little patience. Let your words be seeds, flourishing from simple shells to solid vines. Allow for pruning, shaping, growth.

When devotion ceases to be relevant to you, you move into an abiding creative spirit as well—a still patience, an intentional seeing. You become more like God's loving action: making again and again. And that ultimate remaking—God with us, Christ abiding—is that he's attached to the source, the roots—he knows *how* to best prune the branches. We take a similar action to stay connected just as God took action to stay connected to us—to this world—by becoming human, living among us.

You're a co-creator—making your image alive in the world. Adding to this world your own thumbprint, your distinctive identity, your evident iconography. Just as God did in making each of us. Your image is made real through your words, written down.

Ever been stung by a flippant thing someone said to you? Ever been encouraged by an attentive stranger? This is what's really happening there: a living presence of words is entering into communion with who and what you are—with the words of your being.

That's the power of language:

to warp, destroy, or annihilate

    or

to shape, create, and incarnate.

Make no mistake:

it's nothing less. ○

{ exercise 9 }

Go to the nearest window and take a look outside. What do you see? There are a lot of things out there—visible and invisible—that make up your daily experience, this moment. Nature and all its myriad brilliances: the constant communion you have in the world.

Make a list of what you readily see—the things that stick out most. What are they? Can you name them specifically? What are the names of the trees? Buildings? The flowers? Signs? The stones? Sidewalks?

_____

_____

_____

_____

Now, make a list of what you can't see but what must be out there. Things small, fragile, quiet, obscure. What's imperceptible to your experience that's outside that window, and how are you connected to it?

_____

_____

_____

_____

Reflect on what it's like to pay attention to a world you see every day, but never stop to notice.

_____

_____

_____

_____

_____

_____

_____

_____

_____

_____

10 | counting

Our days may come to seventy years—
or eighty, if we have strength;
yet the best of them are but trouble and sorrow,
for they quickly pass, and we fly away . . .
Teach us to number our days aright,
that we may gain a heart of wisdom.

Relent, LORD! How long will it be?
Have compassion on your servants.
Satisfy us in the morning with your unfailing love,
that we may sing for joy and be glad all our days.
Make us glad for as many days as you have afflicted us,
for as many years as we have seen trouble . . .

May the favor of the Lord our God rest on us;
establish the work of our hands for us—
yes, establish the work of our hands.

—PSALM 90:10, 12–17

What could your life look like if you had a way to count out the person you're becoming?

The psalmists again deliver an imposing message—that even in the sorrows and tragedies of our lives, even in the heat of God's anger and our distress—we are charged to *remember*. The realization of our life's breathlessness is the key to moving into something greater than ourselves, moving into what's beyond knowledge. That's where the heart of God is, right? Beyond knowledge is faith, is wisdom, is a new kind of clarity.

By making manifest our thoughts, intuitions, and lives in poetry, we open up the door to wisdom. In bringing our words to life on the page, we begin to create, cultivate, and realize the time and space we occupy. We live little lives, and there is nothing wrong with it.

By making manifest the things inside us, we're opening ourselves to an array of intricate and constant actions that make God God—the motions of creating. God doesn't create out of devotion to some ideal, cause, or goal. God's desire to create comes from the joy that presents itself in the act of making. Creation is an act of devotion, but devotion isn't a contingency to creating—that's the false dichotomy of the individual who makes with some evangelistic thrust, some imposition to the art being its own end. It's a mode of creating that many believers get lost in—to assure rather than awaken, to convince rather than compel, to induce rather than ignite. Creativity is a mode of being, not just doing. We should want to leave the simplistic arc of being devoted. From this second to the next. From this word to that.

And as the source of our abiding, love is an allegiance that itself warrants creation: the union of people to make pregnancy; the openness of our arms to accept strangers to make a fuller family or community; the pen to the page, brush to canvas, chisel to stone; the giving of our goods and resources; forgiving one another and seeking reconciliation.

All things that bring Christ's love into the world and bind us to one another are art; all works of art are deeper and more complex than the simplicity of obligation. That creation—that incarnating—brings God's love and peace here and now, God's Kingdom. And the tough thing about kingdoms is that they're communities, vast and varied——multivalent, not monochromatic; multiple, not monolithic. We have to learn to live together.

Where there is love and peace, God's kingdom is creating itself over and over, in us and in the world. Sure, you can choose to create nothing in your life, never exploring this ultimate facet of God's character, and you might be able to enter a devoted life. Or—with boldness—you can enter the creative heart of God and begin to live as God lives—attentive, resting in God's enduring Spirit.

What will you leave behind once you're gone? Take that any way you'd like. Is it possible that the *poemia* of your life might make some small difference? What does it declare? What can come from what you've been making this week? A tidal surge in your ocean, drops of rain on the surface of your lake. Either way you make waves, and those waves fan out and move beyond you.

Who are you to say what your life means? Who are you to say what it should be? ∞

{ exercise 10 }

Take some time to write about your first kiss. Bizarre request, isn't it? That moment and that person are significant place-holders in your life. The flutter, the excitement, the tension, the fear, the awe—all of it the stuff of great poetry.

If you're writing this and have not been kissed, write about the anticipation of this event in your life, or what it might feel like to be kissed. Write about your ideal scenario here. Imagine it, envision it, allow its burning in you to come forward and describe itself. If your first kiss wasn't a welcomed one, write about that as well. Do your best to be honest to your memory, however painful to recall; try to make sense of how that experience has shaped your life, what you might say about that cruelty now, what might have happened.

These requests might make you uncomfortable, but maybe that discomfort should be explored. These private things aren't for the world, so you don't have to share them. But it will be good for you to see these things on a page, to capture them for yourself, to live in them, even just for a little while.

So take some time and reflect on that moment. Tell about the surroundings. Where were you sitting? What was your posture? How were you leaning differently into the world? How did you change? Dig out the details.

Chances are that memory is pretty far back in your mind, so it may be a bit spotty. Where you can't remember details, infer them. It's okay to imply in poetry—remember, you're going for truth, not simply honesty. What were the events that led up to the moment? What did it feel like? How did you feel when it was over? Can you describe the face of the person who kissed you?

Now describe—again using sensory details—what it felt like to kiss that person. Infer more if you have to. Really pay attention to the memory here. If you can focus, your mind will bring back things you never knew you could remember. Go on, journal about kissing. It'll make you more human. Don't be shy—risk it, feel it, allow it.

{ exercise 11 }

Reflect over a time when you could clearly feel the presence of God. But don't just record the events—tell the story, relive the story, let it resonate in your being and on the page. Here's a tip on how to make that happen: spend some time setting the scene, letting the details emerge in your mind. Use words you might not use in everyday speech—give the narrative a flare and finesse by paying specific attention to surroundings, feelings, and sensory details. Once finished, read the meditation, but be sure to take your time on the writing.

11 | one summer

Near my home there's a nature preserve right in the middle of the city. It isn't huge by any stretch, but it's big enough—a few winding trails that crisscross, several markers along dirt cuts with features of the area's biodiversity—tree types, rock forms, etc.—and some bridges back and forth over a wide creek whose small tributaries are often dried out and cracking. It's a little ecological gem right in the middle of our move-along metropolis.

Whenever I feel overwhelmed with life—the circumstances of my personal world, or the world at large—I walk the trails for a couple hours. I spend silent time looking through trees, at lizards slinking away over rocks, at the thick bushes of flowers lining parts of the trail—blue bells and orange tiger-striped horns.

Once I was walking this trail with my children when my daughter did something unexpected. We were clipping along when—walking just ahead of us—she stopped suddenly. Her brother and I stopped too, since she'd commandingly put out her arms. She whipped around and whispered loud to us—as kids often do—putting her finger to her lips: "Shhhhhhh, quiet!" And we became so, all of us standing still in the sounds of the small forest: echoing bird songs and the slight snap of animals combing the woods. We stood there for a long time. My daughter then whispered, "Hear God?"

We were moving so fast I had stopped paying attention, but then my little girl helped me see it clearly. I could hear the heart of God pumping its eternal quiet, however faint. I slowly moved to kneel down in front of her and look her in the eye, and she put her little hand on my shoulder. I'm not sure how long our family stayed there, but it wasn't long before a jogger came up from behind us and the moment evaporated into air, snapping us out of our accidental meditation. We kept on down the trail, the small, sacred exchange pumping in my blood. I recited to myself some poems I know by heart, some lines from Psalm 104: "How many are your works, O Lord! In wisdom you made them all; the earth is full of your creatures. / There is the sea, vast and spacious, teeming with creatures beyond number—living things both large and small."

I could try to spend my life in that peace of observation, but I don't think I'm meant to. Many people say that they feel God all the time, that they experience him often. And I don't mean to question their experience when I say that that has not been mine. I guess I experience God in small fragments, like pieces of a puzzle—I keep adding bits over time, trying to build some crisp image, some strong picture. And every time I add a piece to the picture, I find it looks different than I remember, or that it isn't quite what I expected to remember. As if God is inviting me to understand that my life is an intimate and fragile string of connections, as if God and I have been holding hands for a long while, and I'm just coming to realize it—the wonder of God's creation kissing my experience so simply that only in calm, only in peace, can it be discovered.

It's here I begin my belief, in the space of that little unnoticed intimacy, where my momentary piece of the picture is small enough for me to see it clearly. I suppose that in many ways, I stand against seeing the big picture the way many people claim or want to.

By quiet observation, we bear a connection to our origins, however distant or obscure. But the connection isn't rooted in abstractions—instead it's imminent, tangible, full of dust and wood and water and light.

That's the job of the poet: record *that* reality, write down bewilderment and awe— make it known in a way that honors the reality itself by words. Poetry asks me to be content in my littleness, my humble place. Poets must believe in what they cannot see, and the little intricacies in us that create clarity: the vastness of a deliberate world.

From this earth—up from this earth our bodies become. Elements and flecks of interstellar powder that make the heavens also make our shells—houses for bones, but also something like divinity. It's our shared nature to be made by the same holy ingredients. Our smallness is real and it's what makes us real. Wars, rumors of wars, political chaos, economic tragedy—these things seem distant in the face of such vastness.

This natural peace is a kiss from the divine—to know littleness and breathe it in, to feel the hand of a girl holding your shoulder. It's a peace I can't come to without the world, and yet it is of course beyond it. Peace I can't see but only experience; peace alive in me: wild, bare, and from the ground. ∽

12 | something like incarnation

Behold, I will create
new heavens and a new earth.
The former things will not be remembered,
nor will they come to mind.
But be glad and rejoice forever
in what I will create.

—Isaiah 65:17–18

Mornings are best if you're looking to experience quiet. People of faith have known this for a long time—times of prayer and contemplation are fuller when the mind is fresh. And many of the best poets know it as well. The morning calm comes forward from last night's noise—sit meditative, focused, new.

This is the best time to write. In fact, you miss a peace when you sleep through the morning. Yes, sleeping is peaceful, but it's passive peace—you don't choose it, you don't experience it—you live through it, unable to acknowledge the moments it fills. But the quiet of the morning is peace that you live *in*. As Christ is *in* this world, he's in *this* place. He's in it everywhere—in the ever-expanding space above you, the tiniest ticking from the clock, the coughs and creaks of this space settling.

God *loves* this world. God loves *this* world.

And Christ is God's definitive act of creation, God's decisive poem, God's reaching out for us. Think about the physical beauty of it—God becoming human and living in our world. God's revising character, a reorientation of vision toward being what's created. That's the poetry of God.

And that same poem is written in you day after day after day. And you can write that poem out in your life, both in your actions—what Christianity is—and in your language—what Christ is. This is life right now: you and this page. These instruments beside you. The scratching you'll make after these sentences stop.

Is this easy? No. Should it be? No. If it were easy it wouldn't be worth your time, energy, and concentration. Is it fun? Well, sometimes no. But that's not the right question to ask. Fun isn't a measure of anything permanent. It's the measure of something at the surface, of something that will be lost. Ultimately, fun creates happiness, which doesn't sustain us.

Joy is something else. Making is a joy—a sustained way of being in the world where feeling matters less than action, where you choose to live awake, seeing the full horizon of experience and your place in the world—beauty and horror alike. Joy reaches into the earth of you and sets itself for good—a taproot punching through the soil of your becoming, your *poemia*. That's what we should be asking: Is this joy? Is creating joy? Yes. Yes it is.

It's a joy to bring life into the world, just as God did. And when you create out of that, you're helping the Kingdom of God take root. You're making the ethereal force of love in the universe grow to a tangible, material presence.

When you write, you create; when you create, you incarnate. And once you've acted to incarnate, your language moves beyond the simplicity of words, of sounds. It becomes seed—fixing itself, breaking open, reaching deeper.

It's pure joy to create and to be in creation. So we go forth and enact change in the world—however small—by creating alongside God. And as God loves his creation, so do we love ours. ❧

{ exercise 12 }

See all those blank spaces? What's stirring in you that you should put down there? What's that absence saying? That blankness is the brilliant glow of potential.

When you read the following word, what object comes to your mind?

freedom

Close your eyes; take a breath. Focus. What emerges? Say the word to yourself until something comes. Write it.

_____

Journal about that association. What exactly do you see? Describe the image as best you can. If you see a tree, tell about the branches and the bark. If you see a car, what kind and color? Why do you think you see *that* particular object? Your mind has anchored a meaning to that image—a deep-seeded significance that you'd do well to explore.

_____

_____

_____

_____

Now that you've written about the significance of the thing, dig. Dig into your mind for all the moments you can think of that involve that object, that image. What are some memories that contain the thing you've associated with the word *freedom*? There might be many. Chances are that there are only one or two really significant ones. Perhaps the tree is the place you'd go hide as a child after being afraid, after an altercation in the home, to feel safe. Perhaps you remember your father working on his car after work every day—tinkering in which he was easily absorbed.

Go. Tell those stories here. Write without regard to shame, frustration, fear, guilt; think less about quality and more about honesty. Be bold and real. Be you. Your life is one on-going gift of words—say them into the world by writing them on this page.

13 | something like offering

They have no speech, they use no words;
no sound is heard from them.

—Psalm 19:3

No matter what anyone has said to you, your voice matters. And, better still, it's an instrument of grace given to you so that you might create, make, bring hope, bear witness—so that you might more fully realize your life, not some frail self-actualization, but a movement into the larger Kingdom of God.

It's why we speak at all. Your time here is given for you to practice an essence of abiding creativity—an enriched practice that moves beyond devotion and asks you to believe in what you cannot see—the evolution of a miracle, blindness becoming sight.

In the coming moments, when you put that instrument to the page, you're stepping *toward* some heaven, *toward* Incarnation, *toward* the New Creation. Many people choose to live their lives like this—where they stand on the edge of completeness, glimpse paradise in blinks. There is no voice that is not heard.

On the other hand, many people live their lives waiting for something to happen that never seems to happen—they devote their lives to preventing messes, restraining who they could become for fear. These people are stepping *away from* some hell, *away from* Annihilation, *away from* Destruction. Many people live their lives like this—where they step back from being whole, keeping their eyes closed. There are voices they will never hear.

The irony is in the action. One abandons the self for radiance. The other cautiously clutches fear. The first sees the world as opening to the possibilities of faith, hope, love, peace, and joy. The second only sees what the world has come to represent, what it becomes if we don't regard it as beloved, sacred, and eternal creation.

We *make* things the way they are—regard or ruin them. We have the power to create or destroy, to cultivate something sacred or crush it to profanity. Our God made all of *this* holy, and it was made holy by words.

You have, simmering inside, that same intentionality, that thriving capacity, just like God in action. You have that mysterious forest of eternity living in you, so seek it in peace. What you speak onto this page is sacred, and nothing less—a bringing of God into the world. A ringing of your unique voice, an image of a creator, an icon written to one created. So stack your stones today in confidence that nothing you can do will make God love you or this world more or less. Your words go out to the ends of the earth.

When you create today, speak in a language you understand, don't punch it up too much—say it naturally. Resist the temptation to sound grandiose, lavish, impressive, inspiring. Sharpen your words. Clarify. Make the world more tangible, less lofty. Tell about what the actions of the world mean, or could mean.

You're revising your devotional time into something new, something closer to seeking, to regarding.

Think of it like this: you can say vaguely . . .

> "the wind is blowing outside through the trees"

or you can say it with attention . . .

> "by where the road forks, the wind is bending back the arms of the tree, whipping, furious—bending isn't weakness but humility."

Which seems more alive? You have your normal day-to-day life to be terse, brief, static, laconic—to resist entering the mystery. But your spiritual life—your times with God—can be full of the abundant language poetry has to offer, can be full of opening, narrow gates. Your words must honor the world. Again, is the above good or bad? It doesn't matter—it's there, and it's complete as it is. Worry about the good of the thing long after you've written it so that you don't get distracted from this movement.

God speaks through the honest admissions and ecstatic praise that the psalms contain, or the motion, rawness, and visionary witness of the prophets; the depth and width of praise and lament, the gentle balance on which the compass needle rests.

These are actions of *being*, not doing—your spiritual life is an action of being, not doing. It's meant to be complex, but not convoluted; various, but not too complicated; map-able, but still wilderness. Just like poetry.

Your words have life and being, their own rivers and trees, their own light and shadow—they are living words. And the absence of your words, your voice—when placed perfectly—can have the reverberation. In this way, poetry isn't an act of prayer, but an act toward praying—the focused attention of holy language. We use words to get to prayer, but just as often we can use silence. Veneration has many faces.

So now, use your words to make something—a reflection, a vibrant breath, a praise, lament, or observation—bring yourself out. ◡

{ exercise 13 }

Today, we're going to make some lines, or at least make ingredients you'd need to make some lines: similes. While they might be the easiest kinds of metaphors to write, they can be pretty exciting, and even quite powerful, if you really try to make creative comparisons.

For this exercise, you're going to create seven similes. In each sentence you'll compare two dissimilar things using *like* or *as*. For example . . .

> Jennifer cried hard over losing Vic, so much so it was like a thunderstorm coming from her eyes.

Is this a great simile? Nope. It's cliché—comparing tears to heavy rain—and generally non-descript. It *tells* us plenty, but *shows* us little. And people like to be shown, not told. Don't you? Maybe this is a better example . . .

> The seagull let out a deep and terrible squawk, like a rusted nail pried from an old board.

Much better—an accurate comparison of sounds, a simple connection that's a bit unexpected.

Go as far with this as you'd like—take risks, describe in strange ways, try to connect things that aren't normally connected in your mind, or even in the actual world. That brain of yours is doing interesting work in that head of yours—whirring, making, filing, associating. Allow those little instances to emerge in a creative way here.

Some advice: try to stay away from comparisons that you know, that seem familiar. So don't choose the first thing that comes to your mind—choose the third or fifth thing that comes to your mind. You'll make the connections more interesting that way. If you do that, your similes might be a bit weird, but they'll be unique and provide you more space for exploration later.

So get to it—tinker, scribble, cross out, revise. Dirty up the page with your script . . .

Write a simile about *bread* . . .

_____

Write a simile about *kneeling* . . .

_____

Write a simile about *chewing* . . .

_____

Write a simile about *swallowing* . . .

_____

Write a simile about *praying* . . .

_____

Write a simile about *darkness* . . .

_____

Write a simile about *grace* . . .

_____

14 | note

*For **we** are God's* poemia, *created in Jesus Christ to do good works,*
which God prepared in advance for us to do.

—Ephesians 2:10

This world teems with God's living plan, and you're in the middle of it. All of us are created to breathe, and walk, and interact—live out our lives with one another. We're not solitary strangers, but familiar ones.

Even now there's a connection between us: these words. We're growing closer together through this page. Across time and distance, we're now attached—a story larger than us unfolding itself. Another community comes to life. Where two or more are gathered, right?

Words are inviting you into this communion. Your words are realizing a kind of skin—telling your story, witnessing your world, making manifest the mystery of faith:

> Christ has died;
> Christ is risen;
> Christ will come again.

Each word we make moves us toward redemption; whether we believe that or not matters little. And the redemption of you is a kind of poetry. Poems are made by people who've trained themselves to sense, use, and understand words. We write the lines of our lives down, and those lines wander their way into the world, almost always unnoticed. But that doesn't lessen their value—it teaches the poet to see, postures her to hear, gifts him to understand his experience not in a special way, but in an awakened way. So-called poets have simply chosen to write out the life inside them—the poem already existent, alive: breathing within.

So our creativity is a way forward—taking things unseen and making them evident. Creativity is the spiritual practice of moving from within to without, from the solitary to the communal. When God creates, words are the medium. Those words are poetry. Those poems lead to creation. Creation leads to incarnation. Incarnation leads to communion. Communion leads to the new Kingdom coming. The body meeting itself anew.

If creativity isn't a form of faith, I don't know what is.

It's sad that some Christians put too much emphasis on theology and doctrine, on ruling and regulating and deconstructing the mystery of God, experience, and behavior. This sense of understanding God—and being—is a rigidly corrupt mathematics rather than a vibrantly worshipful awe. It's a divorce from all that's creative, and it's ultimately damaging to the image of the God they proclaim. This kind of thinking neglects the elegance of imagery for the grammar of the cerebral—a skin of clearly rendered ideas lacking blood and bone, eyes and ears, breaths and a beating heart. In this we're lost, fundamentally framed and mastered by the limits of the mind rather than the wings of the imagination.

We don't need a conclusive faith, but a creative one—one that can imagine radical grace and peace, one that can co-author and commune, one that can change the world right here, right now.

In us is an energy we're hoping to explore, not necessarily comprehend. It's why glissading notes of a piano pack emotional electricity—why music itself can move us, regardless of words. Why a sound without meaning can chill us. How we can love one another without knowing one another.

Here our words are rising to name and give voice to our experience—not vulgarly qualify or control, but vibrantly redeem and render. The light of who we are refracted on the page, dwelling here—seen through the prism of your words. Right now.

These are songs we can't completely sing, stillnesses we can't completely feel—that's where our language lives, where our truest selves rise from oblivion. Just beyond us. Breathing where we move, moving where we breathe.

Our words in peace. Some wilderness. Something like a song. ⌒

{ exercise 14 }

Go back through this week's notes and underline some stand-out phrases, ideas, intro-spections, similes—what words seem to be emerging as leaders in your writing? What ideas seem to be repeating, opening, allowing themselves? What memories seem significant to you? What parts of you are presenting themselves again and again?

Think hard about it—don't give up easy. Unraveling the impulses and inclinations of your mind is tough work and needs some stick-to-it-ness. All of the things written this week have come from the same mind, so there are threads to pull, even if they're tiny. Remember, loose connections often work best because there's more room for interesting connections to rise up, more room to play. Make at least five notes here:

_____

_____

_____

_____

Now that you've spent time undoing some of your memories, we're going to try weaving something new and different from those seemingly incongruent threads. **Again, you're going to write a ten-line poem. The poem must include at least three similes (*not* ones you've already written!) and utilize the notes you jotted above.** Try to sum up their connection in one word—write it here:

_____

That's the title of the poem you write below.

Oh, and one last thing, one of the poem's similes must be about kissing. Maybe compare an object to someone you've kissed. Maybe compare a sound or feeling to a kiss. Maybe compare your longing for a kiss to some visage in the natural world. Okay, that wasn't the last thing—this is: no rhyming.

Still having trouble thinking of how to begin? Here's the first line, but only if you need it. And it's the last one you're gonna get!

There are times when reaching out your hand is the only thing you can do.

{ 3 }

Was Blind

This morning, a spider crawled under a clover twice its size
and nature had said all it needed to.

We're all hiding, together. The dust of our progress,
the dust of the earth. How should we wait?

Our lives keep beginning to matter, as if
we're all meeting one another for a second time.

The sun comes forward—an orchestrated prayer—
after snow rehearses what it will mean to become water.

The eaves can't take many more of these messages,
waking to a white world with secrets safely hidden.

A fire to swallow us whole; an incident so we can say it right.
These passwords reverberate away in air—never remembered.

We're all meeting under a banner that knows
we've been loving one another since birth.

There are words we haven't ever made with our mouths,
but that we built with our hands.

There's a reason you arrived at this flickering moment—
can you count out stars by shutting your eyes again?

15 | motion

Be still, and know that I am God.

—Psalm 46:10

Just as there's a difference between happiness and joy, there's a difference between being stationary and still.

Stationary is one hang-up after another, a self-sabotage, a series of decisions made from fear of the world, or from being overcome by the world's cruelty—stationary is an affliction.

Stillness is another animal altogether. You aren't moving, but it's immobility with a purpose. Stillness is a decision in spite of the world's standards of being, despite its assaults, pressures, and norms—a bold way toward loving one another through a posture of peace, balance, and patience.

We choose to be stationary or we choose to be still.

The stationary pilgrim always turns his head around to see what was or what could have been. He loses focus on the potential and possibility of now. So he stays in the position of inaction because he can't imagine another way. Stationary is frail-boned, a faint pulse.

The still pilgrim is engaged in a fully-realized act of re-imagination. She's looking down the barrel of the possible—of the moment—and lives by keenly seeing the potential of an enlarging world. She's a revelator ordaining—with courage—an all-surpassing peace. Stillness has clarity in its bloodstream and intention in its heart.

If this is the case, it's best to begin each day slowly waking up to the stillness of the world—it could be the best grace we've been given, or allow. Slowness allows us to enter being still—lets us see through fog or fire, allows for the world to collect itself around us, gives intention the chance to see itself in the mirror, looking back. Slowness allows us to see the world as whole.

Maybe you aren't moving slowly enough if you can't see yourself in the completeness of the world around you. Be still and know.

Writing is an act of slowness: reflectively still and potently quiet. It's an act that helps us come to an understanding of who and what we are by way of creating. When we make something small each day, we start to see that what we make will never be as complete as what's already been made, as creation itself.

In this way, we learn about grace through imperfection, not perfection. And what you're about to make today—your small offering of words, the poem and story of your life—is not perfect.

Grace destroys perfection by making it obsolete—by making perfection a grotesque cheat, a mundane avenue to joy. Far more compelling is our capacity to choose grace for ourselves and pass its loving shadow on to others.

Sure, we understand grace better by knowing that we aren't perfect and God is—this demands little of our imagination. But more radically, we can grow into seeing the world vividly, because the Word of God came *here*, because of the Word's revision to *now*. God is no longer interested in black-white contrast; instead God invites us into coloring clarity.

There's no more clarifying an act than creation, and there's no clearer act of grace than God coming into the world so we might realize the potential of the world God made, and be recreated in it.

If we hold on to our perceptions of imperfection, of short-coming, of incompleteness, we live a simplistic spiritual life rooted in what we *were*, not what we've *become* or what we're *becoming*. If you concentrate on what you lack in this reality, then you'll miss the grace of this instant, and every instant after. And your view of God, your spiritual growth, and your being will never eat solid food. Be complete.

It's possible to go through this dazzling life with only the most rudimentary understanding of God's love in it.

Christ's grace isn't simply about reconciliation with God, but about reordering the priorities and economies of our hearts. God alters everything, physical and spiritual:

physically by the willingness of God to die a human death, to break the body. And spiritually by the recreation of our hearts and renewing of our minds—by our reorientation to what is holy and complete.

When you act from this grace and not a standard of "perfection," you embody the action of stillness—you move beyond your own assertions and words into a completeness of language—the word and breath of God.

This is the slowness we write toward: an amiable reality, a living way—a place in you alive with being. A place in your being thirsting for love in the world. A place that accepts the beauty and unpleasantness of the reality that God so loved. ↜

{ exercise 15 }

Re-read the poem that begins this week's series of meditations. This poem is a bit tougher than the two others. What do you think makes it that way? What does the poem seem to be about to you?

_____

_____

_____

_____

_____

By now, you're a bit more familiar with some of the nuances of poetry—you've been steeped in it for two straight weeks!—and should have a better grasp on experiencing poems. So answer this: What feeling does the poem evoke? Is it an unsettled feeling or a contented one? Why do you think that is? What words, phrases, and images stick out to you? And why are these associations important? Where do they come from?

_____

_____

_____

_____

And another thought: If you were writing this poem, and wanted to make a reader feel the way you feel, what might you do differently? What images might you use to create that feeling? What words? How might you break the lines and keep the pace of the poem congruent with that feeling?

_____

_____

_____

_____

_____

Last one: Now that you've been moving through this book and allowing words to move into your neighborhood, what do you think that poetry is _for_? What is its purpose, as far as you can discern? What are some things that you think a good poem should _do_? There's no wrong answer here.

_____

_____

_____

_____

_____

16 | get out

Glorious and majestic are his deeds,
and his righteousness endures forever.

—PSALM 111:3

When we choose to observe, we choose to pursue what's unlimited; we choose a life of seeking. This is where the world begins opening before you—your life folding and unfolding over and over again. Each moment of each day that puts you in the place where you're sitting right now is exactly the same but completely different—life's little arrangements and variations, whole in their own uniqueness.

This is the unlimited beauty of the world God made: the world "God so loved"—the one the psalmists say God "clothed with splendor" (104) and arrayed with "glorious and majestic deeds" (111)—is waiting for you right now, living, being, and breathing.

These motions—our feelings and experiences—aren't good or bad, however hard that may be to hear. We make them that way, qualify them, compartmentalize them. If we can be trained to think and observe past the black and white of the world, we can begin to enter the imagination. We can render the world with words, experience it through language, and—eventually—see the poetry in it.

For that we must slowly walk the forests of our lives and look around—come alive to the possible and seemingly impossible in each step forward. Today you will speak for the world. Today you will give voice to every part of you that cannot speak. Remember, we live in a world that God called *good*. And that world is the place where we *experience*—pain and joy, chaos and elegance, noise and silence.

Can you make the poem of your life emerge by putting a piece of your life on the page? Every day since you began here, you've been doing just that. Look what you made just yesterday? Is it significant? No, not in the grand scheme, but it's what actually *is*—not an imposed fantasy, not a long-away wish. It's original, special, unique—the world through your exclusive eyes. And that's what makes it lovely.

Your singular vision of the world has no other way of coming out unless you allow it. Maybe every day is supposed to be a road less traveled. Maybe where you are and what you are doing this day is exactly right.

A poem of you—precise, perfect, whole. ∽

{ exercise 16 }

Wherever you are right now, get up and go outside. Find the nearest exit and go. If it's raining, bring a raincoat; if it's cold, bundle up. You're going to go sit outside for ten minutes. And you're going to be writing.

You may be shaking your head right now—laughing, resisting. That's fine—your loss. There's something happening out there, waiting for you to see it. It's something you can't come by trapped in the walls around you—sure, they might wall off the elements, but they also box you in. If you're going to opt out, just stop here and journal—journal, but know that you'll be missing something small and significant.

Walk out—away from your home, away from that special space—and walk right up to the place where the street, sidewalk, road, or scrap of land moves from being "private" to being "public"—where the walkway meets the sidewalk or the driveway meets the street. Go out there and wait, breathe, notice. Keep your eyes open, keep your head clear and focused on the world around. Look. Sit and pay attention to the world as you're still in it—all the details.

Bring the book and your pen or pencil with you. After your ten minutes of observation, pull out the book and get writing. Try to track the small details of the things you've taken in—the colors of cars, the shape of branches, the color of the sky, the sounds of the day, the faces of people, the taste of the air, the smell of the wind.

Take a seat outside somewhere, flip the page, and try to see in a way you've never seen before. Record every element you possibly can.

What are you waiting for? Get going! Wait on no one!

17 | cycle

Remember your Creator
in the days of your youth,
before the days of trouble come
and the years approach when you will say,
"I find no pleasure in them"—
before the sun and the light
and the moon and the stars grow dark,
and the clouds return after the rain;
when the keepers of the house tremble,
and the strong men stoop,
when the grinders cease because they are few,
and those looking through the windows grow dim;
when the doors to the street are closed
and the sound of grinding fades;
when men rise up at the sound of birds,
but all their songs grow faint;
when men are afraid of heights
and of dangers in the streets;
when the almond tree blossoms
and the grasshopper drags himself along
and desire no longer is stirred.
Then man goes to his eternal home
and mourners go about the streets.

Remember him—before the silver cord is severed,
and the golden bowl is broken;
before the pitcher is shattered at the spring,
and the wheel broken at the well,

and the dust returns to the ground it came from,
and the spirit returns to God who gave it.

"Meaningless! Meaningless!" says the Teacher.
"Everything is meaningless!"

—ECCLESIASTES 12:1–8

How will your story find the rest of us? You must begin to put it down in your own words.

Private words, at first. But know that your story is tied to mine, and that it will help give me meaning. Your story is also tied to that clerk who bagged your groceries last week, that person who cut you off in traffic the other day, that man or woman scandalized in the news you heard recently, that jogger you saw.

We're all coming together, whether we know it or not.

And our stories must be read to one another, told again—so you can live it twice. But doing this—moving toward realization—will take time, effort, and focus. You must sit down. Maybe being born again isn't just salvation, but a renewal of our words—our stories put down, released.

You must revise the way you live and move and have your being.

You must roll away the stone.

It takes some arrogance, some ignorance, some wisdom, some stupidity, some vision, and some solitude to convince yourself that your life might matter to the world. But if there's a God who came close to us in *this* reality, then your story matters, and your story must be told. Why are you wasting any more time hesitating?

There are so many ways to tell this story—each one in itself is a small proof that marvels are quite real. Think too hard about the meaning of your life and you'll be quickly swallowed into something like an existential vacuum. Think too little, and you'll never live at all.

Think Ecclesiastes here: Life is meaningless. Meaning and meaninglessness hold one another's hands. Our wise seer says that meaninglessness isn't an ultimate damnation but an ultimate freedom.

The poet-king arrives at the idea that the meaninglessness of life is something like a divine kindness—a small way in the large world; we're made of nothing too special, nothing too great. And we're still loved, and still love one another. This is strange, since it gives life a clear meaning, however insignificant it may seem.

It all comes back: cyclical, precise, vivid, and profound. Maybe something like this . . .

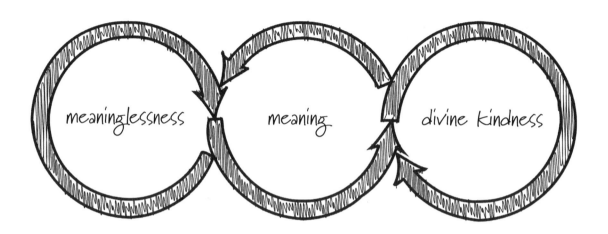

And the cycle goes round and round. We begin full of doubt, negotiate toward acceptance, then move into mystery. We enter meaning through the admission that there's a narrative at work that's larger than any one of us by involving all of us. We're here together, divinely imagined, allowed to live, and revised into a new creation. We're God's spoken words made manifest—divine seeds from humble earth.

Think of it: Just ahead of you there's a completely unknown future—some star waiting to be called forth from the clouds. And just behind you there's a perfectly clear past quickly misting away—dust from the edge of another star finally ending in you.

We are, at every moment, beginning and ending—the star emerging and the star receding. Past and present meeting inside our created and given skin.

What future and what past are you making right now? What light is traveling far to find you? ᴄᴐ

{ exercise 17 }

For today's exercise, you're going to make a vocabulary web. This practice is one that's sometimes used in pre-writing to help an author understand the elements that his or her mind associates with a given subject. In the space provided on the next page, you'll write a word inside the circle—the name (a common noun) of an animal, like a dog, fox, llama, eagle, etc. From that circle you'll draw lines outward and write words, ideas, or brief descriptions that you associate with that animal, no matter how obscure.

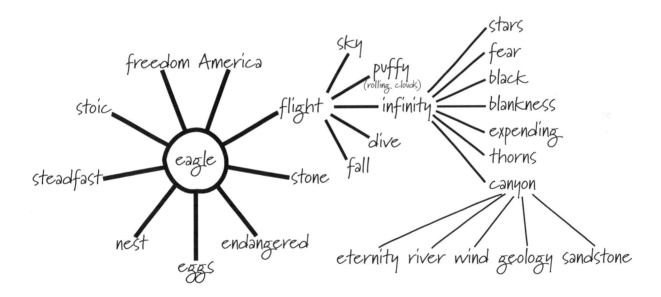

Through this web, you can track your mind's ability to associate words, images, and objects. For example, if you found yourself writing a poem about freedom, perhaps it might be a good idea to use vocabulary that underscores that idea, and to include images that endorse that idea in your mind. You might then choose to include *flight* as a central action in the poem. And you might choose to use images like *stones* or *canyons* because they represent immovable, eternal aspects of the wilderness, a term often associated with freedom. You probably wouldn't choose to use the egg as a central image because it's more representative of fragility than strength, unless there was some animal breaking through that soft shell into the world.

By creating a diagram, you can begin to imagine the endless possibilities of word associations. If you look at the original word and look at the lines leading away from it, you'll eventually come to *expanding*—a broad term that can be used in a variety of ways in a poem but is still connected—however loosely—to the original word, *eagle*.

So here's our exercise: Think about some animals you've encountered or—better yet—continue to encounter in your life. They can't be specifically domestic—they should be wild animals. Make a list of five here:

_____

_____

_____

Now choose one and make a web. What comes to mind when you think of that animal? As usual, there are no "wrong" answers here—just honest ones. Capture those reactions. What does that animal represent? What is it known for? What do you think it means to you? To others? Describe it, its surroundings, its behavior. What feeling does that animal give you?

Your web should contain ten "first generation" thoughts. Then choose three of those first generation words/ideas and add five more words/ideas to make a "second generation" web using the new term. Then choose three of those new terms and add five more to make a "third generation." If you want, you can riff on this endlessly, adding and adding and adding generations. No connotation or relationship is insignificant. All of them have some kind of value. Use all the space—fill up the next page!

Get sketching . . .

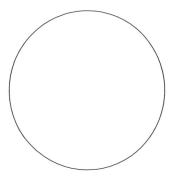

{ exercise 18 }

Reflect on an experience that you've had outside, where the world and nature seemed sacred, beautiful, full, and right. Tell that story below, recalling what details you can. What images and stories from your life come to the fore when you think of your interactions with the natural world? Think of colors, textures, tones—what's preserved? Write them out before you read today's reflection. Don't skimp—give at least two strong paragraphs—really dive into those memories. When you're done, head on to the meditation for the day.

_____

_____

_____

_____

_____

_____

_____

_____

18 | one winter

Each winter, I'm walking outside when a snow storm begins. It's a little arrangement I have with the season—I show up and so does it; we usually meet in a field, lingering in the gray quiet alone. We move through the air together, everything aligned. The bright, furiously elegant silence—a stunning array of white, driving thickness. I'm thankful for this appointment: it helps me open my eyes and really see, to remember that grace is a gift to the world that is free.

Over the years I've noticed that there are certain landscapes that make their way into my writing. My poems, stories, and essays are often centered around forests and fields, and the line where the two worlds meet. Those are my totem landscapes—the edge of mystery where the world unlocks itself, where I commune, where beautiful shadows of forgiveness and grace stir.

One walk in late February years ago it happened. When winter and I had our little meeting, I was on the cusp of a big change: I was about to become a father for a second time. I went out to clear my head and give my dogs their daily walk. Gray afternoon sunlight, the two animals off their leashes and running randomly in a field, chasing their own trails. Just a call and they'd pant back to me.

I was making my way up a shallow knoll and around a small pond when the sky opened, bellowed snow. The annual pattern unbroken—I shouldn't have been surprised. I kept walking toward a fence line a few hundred yards off. Once there, I stared into a stand of trees down a long hill, a stone's throw beyond me. The dogs were far in the opposite direction, diving playfully at one another. I began thinking of my unborn boy who would arrive in only a few weeks—his waiting, his small breathing, his forming hands. I thought about the name we would give him.

Then to my right, out from a bend and another congregation of trees, three horses emerged. One stag—huge hindquarters and shoulders, a truly massive coal-black, animal—and two smaller offspring—speckled white and brown, with kind eyes.

Against the fence, they lined up facing me—a child on either side of the father, staring at me through the flakes. I looked down, intimidated, and saw that the dogs had come to mirror the position, one on either side of me. It would have been comical if the quiet of the moment had not been so resonant and clear—a deep gulch around all of us like the calm in a church between the clanging bells to call people to morning prayer. Our breaths visible in air, exchanges of unobtrusive and surreal connectivity— no barks, grunts, or coughs—just clear faces through the snow, realizing all together that our world—this world you're sitting in right now—is bigger than what's seen, any force, trend, event, or sin.

There's a pulse in this world that's always present just below our surface, if only we'd take time enough to touch the skin over our wrists. It's a song we all sing—one hidden hymn of God. And the voice of this song is right where our attentions collide with God's intentions. We're all singing inside the body of God, our voices ringing clear in God's ears.

The horses broke away—turned around and galloped from our gathering, back toward the bare woods scattered in snowfall. The dogs and I stood stunned, not knowing where to go next, now that our connections to one another had been exposed. And I felt a strange newness, a reckless reassurance—feeling whole for the first time in a long time. The words of the psalmists rang in me: "Cleanse me with hyssop, and I will be clean; wash me, and I will be whiter than snow" (51:7).

I remember my first thought after the stillness broke: This is what it must be like inside the womb—safe, still, a complete breath of peace. A strange and surprising thought, but real. A collision between what is and is to come, where we wait antici- pating nothing, not knowing that our perception is going to shift, grow, radically explode.

All the beasts and one song—all of us whole, seeing the beauty in the world God has rescued. Our lives near touching: a boy about to begin, a father's opening eyes. So holy is this world that maybe it's singing right along with us, even if we mistake it and ourselves as voiceless. ᴗ

19 | fragments

When I look at the night sky and see the work of your fingers—
the moon and the stars you set in place—
what are mere mortals that you should think about them,
human beings that you should care for them?
Yet you made them only a little lower than God
and crowned them with glory and honor.

—Psalm 8:3–5 NLT

Is it possible that the observations you're about to read are acts of worship for both of us?

These are some quick jots about the view from my window one morning, taken as-is right from my journal over a few days, hence the lowercase (I don't really care for using capital letters!) and few edits—just raw and real reactions, sensory descriptions, questions . . .

— the horned aloe plant and its jagged green fingers, in the terra cotta pot.

— rust bleeding over the top bar of the fence, almost like spray paint—but something undomesticated and opportune. something wild.

— three saplings the neighbor planted last year rising from the brown grass. i hope they'll survive the winter and give us shade someday.

— their three small shadows and outstretched arms—changing with the sun. by the time i end this sentence those shadows will be different, but only a little.

— a puddle from rain last night pooled in a divot in the pavement. a shallow grove in the stone can hide a universe of life.

— a hole where the dogs have been excavating (against my protests), ready to bury a roast bone from dinner earlier this week.

— the crumpled edge of a gutter pipe—like metal bowing to pray if it were possible—and the shadows of the pine over a bed of cats-paw ivy.

— two empty and decrepit adirondack chairs; stoic stance against the sun coming up. the wood porch could use some upkeep, it won't be long till things really start to fall apart.

— the pine imposes a shadow over part of the yard—bowing out and up.

— beads of rain on the face of st. jude look like tears. do you cry for the way we let go or hold on? the way we forget one another?

— patchwork shadows emerging as the clouds clear, quenched clover clustered together.

— a calico cat is sneaking in the scattered leaves right now. he doesn't know i'm watching. he's focused—hunting just like me.

— the misty dart of a cardinal shooting to the feeder—i wonder where we're supposed to be going, and if we should be going there together.

— does my presence outside this scene make it more or less real? more or less beautiful? what's lost or gained by my seeing?

— stark spears of tiger lilies—they'll yawn open in a month or so, let us look inside for meditations.

— a telephone wire sagging—it can't hold the weight of all the things we've said but never did.

— the wind chimes are still: quiet golden fingers—patiently waiting.

— it's occurring to me: maybe heaven has broken in and i'm just now noticing.

— when i rouse my senses—attend to the lights around me—i begin seeing that i'm living near to both grief and joy.

— this world must realize: even the vast sky is one small detail.

So that's it—nothing too fancy, just some noticed things: thoughts slowed enough to be captured, jotted, rendered. A small snapshot of my backyard—the little life I live—written down for good. There's not much to be told—just ordinary and simple observations said in my own voice, and no one else's.

If you had been here, would you have noticed different things? I'm certain of it. Your eyes inform your vision of the world.

For me, the above notes are worship—witnessing and reaching out to God. Considering the works of God's fingers.

What you read above is a moment that will never come again and never was before— the singular uniqueness of experience, vision, and perception. This is my life, my lens, my world. God has given it to me. And it's my job to care for it, render it gracefully, see it as it's been made—to wholly love the world as God so does.

Here's the beauty in creating and observing every day: The above is the small and living proof that I opened my eyes and was alive in the world, that I saw and didn't flinch. This is my *poemia*.

And what you're about to make below will be the same, and then some. Your jots are the enduring evidence that we collided—that your life and my life are shivering with the same awe and wonder and mystery. That your vision and God's creation came together, that you emulated and acted out of imagination.

You are *here*. This is *yours*.

What do you see? What divine and complete vividness is before you, asking to live forever?

Do you see it now? Beyond the small signal that you were here, beyond our collision, is the truth that you're co-creating—existing in the redeemed world where God still walks.

You're making a pocket-sized reminder of the grace alive in you—that you woke up today breathing the very air God breathed. There's a poem about to emerge. ҩ

{ exercise 19 }

Go ahead, now it's your turn. Imitate what you just read above, but use your world and words to do it. Go outside and sit, or sit near a window. But you can't go to the same place you went a couple of days ago—you'll have to go the *opposite* direction. See if the world looks a little different by contrast. Write what you see, try to qualify it, find those little jewels of reality—natural and unnatural—resting right in front of you. Write at least ten little observations.

Even if it seems mundane, there's a truth living in it. Find it. Make it known.

20 | breathe

And live peacefully with each other.

Brothers and sisters, we urge you to warn those who are lazy.
Encourage those who are timid. Take tender care of those who are weak.
Be patient with everyone.

See that no one pays back evil for evil, but always try to do good to
each other and to all people.

Always be joyful. Never stop praying. Be thankful in all circumstances,
for this is God's will for you who belong to Christ Jesus.

—1 Thessalonians 5:13–18 NLT

You showed up. Here you are again. Are you ready to make an offering?

You take about 28,000 breaths each day. Is it possible to make each one a prayer? Or is each one already a prayer—a sacredness passing from you, unacknowledged?

It's so simple. These pages and their scribbles—light and shadow around you, the unnoticed but familiar noises of your day.

We see. We touch. We smell. We hear. We taste. This life.

Our love for God is rooted in the sensory experiences we have in this world—what God has made here, the creation we experience—and if we can pay attention to what our senses absorb, we can tap out our own small stories in a wonderful way—respectful of the beauty in the world, honoring to what's real, inside and out. If our senses allow us to participate in the world God has made, we find our way through this world to God by attention, by going forward, trusting our senses and experiences.

Do you want to live in peace and hope? It can be simple.

All you have to do to live is insist on staying awake. Don't flinch or fade; don't forget or fake it. Just be. Accept who you've been made to be and let everything you do come from the impulses of seeking that God has placed in you.

Is it possible to lean into God's mystery just so? Enough that you can see the world around you as it was designed? As it has evolved?

Breathe.

Doing this thing—this life—right is about slowing down. Making time still enough so you can say *yes. That's right. There. It is. Right now.*

Breathe.

Know that that breath is giving you life. That that moment was just what you needed. That all of what you have right now in this split second is enough.

Keep going forward, however slow. Be intentional about your thinking, your doing, your being.

Breathe.

Feel your lungs filling up. Who you are—your body and your soul—nourished, like a prayer.

That's God: the graciousness of the immaterial, the matter of the invisible. We owe our bodies to the mystery of life. Particles of God's presence filling us like air.

Is there a time where you might see your life new? Will you let God transform your moments into some new and lovely whole? Some holy string of poetic breaths?

God has affirmed creation and its beauty by letting us engage it, manipulate it, remember it. We would do well to preserve it—by our words, our actions, our attitudes, and even our thoughts. This existence—this moment right now—is our past and our future meeting. Our faith and our imagination colliding in the actuality of the world. Those forces lead us to remember what it means to be human, to contemplate how we should live with one another now, and charge us to re-vision our world's potential. God's revelation is one that travels toward the possible, the imminent, the moment *at hand*.

Breathe.

These three modes of your being—past, present, and future—are numbered and totaled in the vessel that you are, the vessel that God made.

Make no mistake about this moment: it's holy and you're in it. By staying awake and witnessing the world, you and God are agreeing to grace. Communing in prayer. Praying without ceasing.

Breathe.

Don't worry or concern yourself with what you're about to make or the quality of what will come out. The person you are right now is just good enough to make the things inside you materialize. Besides, if you don't like it, you can always change it later.

Maybe think of it like this: that light—the light above, behind, beside, or in front of you—shouldn't be the only light in the room. The light inside you matters more than anything. Stop hiding it under the bushel of your need for comfort, solace, pardon, desire, or commitment to an easy faith. Go forward and create.

Breathe.

Work hard enough that you leave the world for a bit, but not so hard that you're removed from the world. This moment would have never happened if you hadn't shown up today.

Breathe again.

Open yourself and begin. ∽

{ exercise 20 }

Today, you're going to fill in the blanks for your exercise. Go through this list as fast as you can, making connections between the ideas in the sentence. As usual, don't worry about weirdness. Just let your mind do the work and see what comes forward . . .

1. Coffee is to awakening as tree is to _____.

2. This morning, my friend woke up with a strange feeling of sadness and _____.

3. I wonder what it must be like to be a _____—there are so many directions to go.

4. When I saw my _____ I was surprised at the way it _____.

5. Jelly is to screws as _____ is to grief.

6. The feeling of _____ was electrifying. I could never imagined that I'd find myself _____-ing that way.

7. It isn't the fear I mind so much, but the constant _____ that comes along with it.

8. There are no ways to describe _____. But I'll try and sum it up with this one word: _____.

9. Could he really be thinking about _____? If so, that means we're _____.

10. If she says, "_____" one more time I think I'll _____.

11. I've counted my _____ so many times that I've forgotten what it means to have so much and so little.

12. Tiger lilies are to _____ as Moses is to _____.

13. _____ is to friction what _____ is to gravity.

14. I was devastated—all the thief took when he broke into my home was _____.

15. I was overjoyed—she surprised me with _____.

16. If I were about to die, I'd like to confess that I _____.

Now, pick three of the most interesting and write about why you like them and why you think you might have chosen to fill in the blanks that way. Anything interesting coming from these connections? Reflect on your associations below.

21 | making new

He who was seated on the throne said, "I am making everything new!"
Then he said, "Write this down, for these words are trustworthy and true."

—REVELATION 21:5

God is in the process of revision. In the cycles and involved dances of this world, and in the quiet revelations and revolutions in our hearts, God is evolving things *creatively*.

God works with words. Think of it as something more like art than theology. Or—better—an imaginative and inventive theology: one that leans into *poemia*. A grace more like artistic action than analytical gymnastics.

Christ's coming into the world is one such move: God comes down from abstraction, revises into tangible human wholeness; Christ is God's inventive regard and reimagining. Words upright and walking—everything in this world about to break open with newness.

Think of the Crucifixion—another act of creative revision. God's body broken—taken apart, its muscle and intricacy exposed. The Word beaten till it's in just the right place to perform its fullest function.

And of course there's a complete remaking in the Resurrection—what was lifeless is now alive and breathing. God's insistent cry that our bodies—that our tiny hulls—are just parenthetical predicaments inside the larger question of the Kingdom of God, and that death is another avenue toward life.

These are God's resounding reversals of power: to rise you must lower; to gain your life you must lose it. And this pattern moves forward, the Kingdom gates opening even as you read this sentence. Maybe God's original intention is the slow and vital stepping forward, the now's and nearly's of our world becoming.

This is the provocative sensibility of revising: the whole created world gets accounted for; everything is redeemed when it's revised. In writing, often revision is a feat dedicated to keeping no one out—the revised poem's horizon broadens. The writer tries his or her best to enlarge the scope of the piece by focusing on the tininess of a word, sentence, or line. And that smallness has drastic implications.

God's reckless grace keeps no one out. It embodies and encompasses. It opens and expands. And it does so by narrowing into death. A creative suicide to saves us all.

Say what you want about Christ, but there's no lack of originality, innovative action, or creative thinking. Christ's presence in the world is a revised reality, a new wholeness, where the old has gone and the new has come, where our standards and ways recalibrate to a humility of being and stillness. And God's Spirit is doing the same in us, for the sake of this world.

The act of creating and revising, then, is an act of unpretentiousness. Putting down words on this page requires an attention to the small, the insignificant, the intricate. It's a small picture that we paint.

It's just such with our faith life, too: we must become what God is making, what God is remaking. You must become God's *poemia*.

Bear yourself before the page, wait, be patient. Ask for something impossible. Come to the desk for renewal.

If we say to God *use my words*, they'll be made into poetry. If we say to God *use my life*, it will be revised into a risky, unimaginable grace. A life with Christ is a vocation of attention and peace. This moment—just like all of the others you've had—is a stake in the ground to mark your renewal. This moment could be the most significant revision of your life.

But the thing is, revision is never-ending. It's a constant awareness of and toward a fullness of being—a movement into mystery of who God is in the world where you live. God is making all things new.

You have to ask to awaken; you have acknowledge to arise.

God can make your fragmented narrative an elegant poem; God can make your simplistic existence a resounding completeness.

Be born again. And again. And again. And again.

Each time you ask, the lilies of this moment are opening. And everything is being made new. ⌒

{ exercise 21 }

All of these days culminate right here—you're now thinking like a poet. Maybe you've even found yourself doing it during your normal day—hearing words and associating them with others, moving between ideas and thinking of how they might work in other contexts. Heck, maybe you even want to jot down ideas you think of hoping to work them into something later. All of that's great! Maybe you should start carrying a little pad and paper in your pocket so you can make a quick note and revisit it later. Geez, you're such a geek!

Again, go through the week's scribbles and pull out the stones you think can be smoothed into gems. Trust your instincts and your nerves. What you're trying to make in this world isn't perfect, just complete. No jewel is flawless, and the flaws that a jewel does contain give it personality. Be all right with effort.

Write a ten-line poem that uses an animal as its central image. Make sure that it's a personal poem that somehow taps into the metaphorical meaning of the chosen animal, not simply a poem about seeing an animal. Connect it to the events of your life—preferably something secretive, private, maybe even provocative. Those things that you hide from the world are always the most interesting, not by some scandal, but because they're strangely special to you, unique to your experience. And again, you should avoid rhyming.

If you're having trouble getting started, go to the poem for this week—"Was Blind"—and steal a line from it to get you going, but do that only as a last-ditch effort—you can write your own lines from here.

_____

_____

_____

_____

_____

_____

_____

_____

_____

_____

_____

_____

{ 4 }

To Mark the Place

Remember that I said this:
maybe the day is just beginning
where belief would end.

Looking back, how would you define it now?
A life revealed in clarity of morning prayer:
scape of dawn, stars receding in thin cloud,
the body bent—request or resignation?

Even if you don't, stars understand.
Lights arriving because their bodies
are already gone—graves always give way to glory.
As if the dark stones over their violet tombs
have rolled back and it's now enough
to make you see what small faith you had before.

Isn't this your devotion?
Place your hand in your pocket
when asked to give.
Give whatever it is you find there.

And if you should pull a dusty seed
place it in the earth.
Forget it came from you.
Never let your left hand know.

So that years from now, following home
those tiny lights some long road back to this place,
you might be surprised to see
your accidental gift revising the horizon—
small green proof that we were here,
that we once crossed this road together.

No record of denials set down;
no crowing uncertainties about it.
And what you once thought anathema
turned into the kindness of incantation.

Maybe what I said before was wrong:
the day is actually ending
where this world will not believe.

22 | the whole world

. . . and he began to teach them.
"Blessed are the poor in spirit,
for theirs is the kingdom of heaven.
Blessed are those who mourn,
for they will be comforted.
Blessed are the meek,
for they will inherit the earth.
Blessed are those who hunger and thirst for righteousness,
for they will be filled.
Blessed are the merciful,
for they will be shown mercy.

Blessed are the pure in heart,
for they will see God.
Blessed are the peacemakers,
for they will be called children of God.
Blessed are those who are persecuted because of righteousness,
for theirs is the kingdom of heaven.

"Blessed are you when people insult you, persecute you and falsely say
all kinds of evil against you because of me. Rejoice and be glad,
because great is your reward in heaven, for in the same way
they persecuted the prophets who were before you.

—Matthew 5:2–12

Every day since I started paying attention to my life—started intentionally contemplating, writing, thinking—I've been offered a small scrap of silence each day. Often it comes when I'm intentionally seeking it, but sometimes it sneaks up on me. I'll be going about my business in all the usual noisy places—work, home (especially after my kids have gotten out of bed!), driving, wherever—and a noiselessness emerges out of the barrage or monotonous background: a few seconds of complete stillness.

These polished quiets are a haven for me—a tiny seclusion from all the flickering busyness. The trick is allowing myself to experience them; I've been so focused on my tasks for the day that I've worked through the moment or I've been so startled by it that I push it away. For me, these flashes of peace are a foil to what's always happening, a reassurance against what's constantly moving around or in me—they're a reminder that there's always a retreat just before me and just after me. When I slow down long enough to feel the reality of quiet—that it's everywhere—a wonderful peace comes and I realize that I'm not living within noises but between silences.

Here's the beauty of the past few weeks: there's new and tangible proof that you've walked the earth, that your life was real; your words bear witness to that—these scribbles of you, these notes and observations are now part of the hope you have.

We've come together, crossed a divide, and opened our eyes just enough to capture the divine beauty in and around us.

Our little experiment: this journaling, these lines of poetry, these moments in your day. You and I are bringing the world together, slowing down enough to see things many people you know have never slowed down long enough to see. This—maybe—is God's intent for our vision: that we have a deliberate and complete peace, a reconciled reality, a whole community, a blessed hope. Maybe that's why Christ charges us to engage the weak, the sad, the starving, the strange—that we might move closer to bearing these realities.

There's a song my wife and I sing with our children to pray—one you probably know—that seems to me to harken to this idea of completeness, of community: "He's Got the Whole World In His Hands." We sing it often in our home with the names of friends and family living in the rhythm:

> He's got Nona and Pop in His hands . . .
> He's got Stacie and Doug in His hands . . .
> He's got Grandma and Grandpa in His hands . . .
> He's got Charlie and Sonya in His hands . . .
> He's got the puppies and fishes in His hands . . .
> He's got the whole world in His hands.

Everyone we know makes it in—at some point—and, of course, there are mainstay names not mentioned above. It once occurred to me that the words say "*whole* world" and I wondered how much we—I, really—actually meant it; maybe we just meant *our* whole world, which misses the point. So we've added a refrain that's become a standard, and we sing it together each time to end the song:

> He's got our neighbors and our enemies in His hands.
> He's got our neighbors and our enemies in His hands.
> He's got our neighbors and our enemies in His hands.
> He's got *all of us* in His hands.

It seems to me that this is our hope, or should be. That when we pay attention, we begin to see what's left out, negated, hidden, or on the cusp of coming forward and that we should reconcile to it.

This might be what Christ is calling us to in the Sermon on the Mount—an inclusive community, a complete and sweeping graciousness. You can't argue with the child-like truth of this kind of revolution, yet you can't quite grasp its fathomless depth either. At least I can't. I intend to spend my whole life trying to come close.

Christ calls us: practice slowness, grip the moment before you and see it without hesitation, see the real and brilliant places before you; love your neighbor, bless your enemy, treat all creation with amiable respect. Because each being in this world is *created, designed, intentional.*

How can we possibly be expected to do these heavy things without times of quiet, solitude, contemplation, and prayer? And how can we reflect on what it means to practice the Way of Jesus if we have no creative means to do so?

The question is simple: how will the world change without you? You're here—built with a purpose, bought with a price. How can you even think about wasting another moment neglecting the grace in this world in favor of its brokenness?

Don't waste one more second of your precious life on that fear, that shame, or that guilt. All those toxic seeds that take root, dig deep.

Get up and walk from here. Forgive those who need forgiving. Apologize to those who deserve it. Reconcile. Or maybe you need to forgive yourself. Do it.

Why waste another second on the small violence in your heart when you can rise to meet a road of peace, when you can pause in a moment where God has come nearer to us? How will you do it?

Have you ever seen dye plunge into water? The way it thins, spinning out liquid tangles—locks and threads—winding in and out of themselves? Try it sometime if you can't see it clearly in your mind. Try it right now.

The color slowly spreads itself, meanders until the glass has tinted. This is what it's like to awaken and see that your words matter, that Heaven isn't far from *right now*, that it's broken into this world and is being realized every moment you, your neighbor, and your enemy breathe the same sacred air. Its colors fanning out, spreading, changing the very tint of existence.

And just like that drop of dye against the water's surface, everything is about to be subtly redefined; everything is about to be new. Every bit of this world revisioned. Every moment remembered. ⌒

{ exercise 22 }

You've almost made it through this little program. Wow—that's a lot of work! Take a second to look back at what you've done for the past few weeks. What do you think? See what you wrote down for the exercise during Day 1? Has writing changed you in any way? Are you beginning to see the world differently? If so, what is it about the act of writing that makes you see the world anew? Do you think that you might want to continue writing after this week is over? If so, how will you go about it? What's your next step? How does the act of writing—and of writing poetry—make you more complete?

_____

_____

_____

_____

Take a look at the poem for this week. Write down some thoughts you have about it. What are some words that come to mind when you read the poem?

_____

_____

_____

_____

Now, go ahead and choose one or two of those words to write about. What story from your own life and experience does that word evoke? Write the story down, and—again—be sure to do the story justice by adequately describing it—sensory details, rich descriptions, care for language. It can be any story that has to do with the word you wrote. Be sure to write at least ten sentences.

Get to it!

_____

_____

_____

_____

_____

_____

_____

_____

_____

_____

_____

_____

_____

23 | basic math

And Mary said:
"My soul glorifies the Lord
and my spirit rejoices in God my Savior,
for he has been mindful
of the humble state of his servant.
From now on all generations will call me blessed,
for the Mighty One has done great things for me—
holy is his name.
His mercy extends to those who fear him,
from generation to generation.
He has performed mighty deeds with his arm;
he has scattered those who are proud in their inmost thoughts.
He has brought down rulers from their thrones
but has lifted up the humble.
He has filled the hungry with good things
but has sent the rich away empty.
He has helped his servant Israel,
remembering to be merciful
to Abraham and his descendants forever,
just as he promised our ancestors."

—LUKE 1:46–55

What will you add to the world today?—it's easier to subtract, break down, negate, detract. But adding, that's our calling—to make the world more alive. Every day, you could make something beautiful if you just paid attention a little more, put forth a tiny bit of effort.

The implications of your faith suggest it should be a *practice* in your life—making for the sake of making. A practice where there's nothing to win, gain, or reap—just the satisfaction of creating. Creating is, after all, your Creator's obsession.

Creating is the ultimacy of any person or group—adding some good to the world. And just as it was the ultimacy of God to begin creating—and eventually reimagining that being, character, and imperative by way of Christ—it's our honor to create as well.

Think of the old commands, one of which is directly about our words: *Don't take God's name in vain*. It's not simply a prohibition, but a comment on intent, and the power of that intent. Because God is with us, it's sinful to misuse our language. Our words—breathed from us—become part of the living economy of the Kingdom of God.

We often choose to destroy that Kingdom—the violences of our hearts and minds come forward in some pretty revealing ways. Those violences were made very real at the Cross; we can see clearly that we're often the ones acting in opposition to creation. We help make the climate of chaos, confusion, and crumbling. Our Annihilation is always the opposite of God's Incarnation.

Then shouldn't we—as Christians—be asking some tough questions?

What practices in my life lead to annihilation, for me or others?

Am I part of a community, cycle, system, workforce, government, or principality that facilitates, participates in, funds, or fosters annihilation, disdain, fear, disparity, or exploitation?

Or, better yet, do I condone by my practices, habits, inaction, or muteness those actions which move against the Incarnation?

Or, take it this way:

Is there a group of people—social or economic—that isn't part of my Christian community because they make me feel uncomfortable? How might they want to be treated or welcomed? What might they need?

Do I know anyone who is part of a group that others around me have grown to scorn, ignore, or disenfranchise? Why might people behave this way?

What am I—and the people with whom I associate—putting into the world and what effect is it having on the humanity and dignity of others, on *the least of these*?

Last, most importantly:

Am I an "enemy" to anyone? Is anyone an "enemy" to me? As a believer, what am I going to do about it?

If I or my faith community have made "enemies" and feel justified in it because of some moral high-ground, popular hierarchy, socially regarded scriptural mandate, or personal opinion, what's the cost to my "enemies" for holding firm that position? What's the cost to me or my community of believers? Or better yet, my enemies?

Which of these positions is most valuable in the economy of God's Kingdom: Rightness or kindness? Correctness or love? Serenity or peace? Morality or charity? Perfection or completeness?

I ask—not out of arrogant knowing, but modest seeking—because I wonder myself. I ask because I wonder if I am living as Jesus would live. Is there a way to love and accept all people in peace, in a way that hopes and strives for change but doesn't risk anyone's humanity—neighbor or enemy—being cast aside? That underscores the God-made image in which we all were made? That exposes injustice, cruelty, disparity, or spiritual arrogance for what it is while offering a way toward reconciliation for all people—oppressors and oppressed?

It seems, in this way, that Christianity isn't so much about standing up for what's right as it is about standing beside liberation, beside grace—which in itself is solely _right_. The Christian can't hold a posture of contrasts as much as a posture of charities. Can we come together in the gift that is the Incarnation to foster a new way to live?

Poetry, in purity, is an act toward incarnating, toward making manifest God in the world. When you're creating, you're moving toward that purity. Making violence of any kind is harder when your daily practices are rooted in making peace.

The Prophets act this way by giving us profound examples of language's evocative calamity—so powerful is their lament that they must make it poetry. Only poetry can do justice to what must be said—it carries the emotional freight, exposes evil for what it is, champions justice and balance, beauty and goodness, and bears witness to all in between.

Our words—our poetry—allow us to see clearly.

Mary sings her poetry. So powerful is her experience that it must be put down in verse to come close to honoring its complexity. Eventually Mary's Song is one of acceptance in the face of what surely must have been awful confusion, dramatic isolation, and fervent fear. Her prayer isn't simplistic praise and gratitude as much as it is a prophetic and uncompromising vision. God is reimagining human community through her womb, through a radical and unstoppable grace. Imagine trying to make sense of that? Then or now.

Our words—our poetry—allow us to cry out vividly.

You've felt like these people, I'd imagine. Afraid, anxious, angry, justified, frustrated, isolated, left behind. Sound familiar? If you've felt that way, what are the chances that you or your community have made others feel that way?

If you're going to bring God into the world, you'd better be ready to become a poet—poised to see, trained to hear, and bravely empathic enough to discern truth from injustice and work toward making it right.

It's not a special skill, but a human obligation. So-called poets aren't born distinct, but awakened to the gifts that have been in them all along. The Christian should be poised to see, but the Christian who chooses to create should be poised to see and tell the truth—now there's an act of co-creation.

Can you give your life away to others? Can you act to help, reaching out with your voice and hands to bring comfort, even when it isn't comfortable? Can you give something away you can't get or take back? ⌒

{ exercise 23 }

React to the following—don't think too hard about it! Just go forward, jot, and focus . . .

1. Choose one of the names of God listed below. Write it out below.

Omega	Fire	Portion	Tower
Scepter	Rose	Diadem	Potter
Sorrows	Physician	Shield	Beginning
Stone	Carpenter	Teacher	Refuge
Foundation	Lamb	Temple	Shiloh
Keeper	Dayspring	Witness	Morning Star
End	Peace	Sophia	Author
Horn	Rock	Vine	Branch

2. Write a statement confessing something you did as a child that no one, or few people, know.

I'm sorry, when I was small I . . .

3. Choose another name of God and write it below. Then address God in a way that opens a conversation—ask a question or make an open-ended statement.

4. Write down a sentence of praise where you compare God—and God's forgiveness—to a natural object.

Because your forgiveness is like _____, I will not fear _____.

5. Now make a statement that seeks closure, but does it in an unexpected or strange way—maybe even a way that contradicts what was said above.

6. Now reflect on a few of the names of God. Which ones stand out? With which do you most identify? Why, do you think? Write down some of your thoughts.

{ exercise 24 }

Before you go on to reflect on today's meditation, write fresh. Below is part of today's exercise. And be sure to save a little time after the reading for some jotting . . .

Think hard and remember one thing you heard yesterday—a phrase, command, string of words, idea—anything really. It can be something said to you directly, overheard; something you read, a flash of words that somehow emerges from the pace of the day before. Write it down here:

_____

_____

_____

_____

Now, think about it a bit. What's the actual context? What will happen to those words if you change the context? How can you change the context? Can you punch up the words a little and tug out something poetic? Is it poetic as is? Rewrite here, changing what feels right to change. Forget about truth for a moment:

_____

_____

_____

_____

Now really go to work on it. Give it a completely new context, introduce a new idea. How would that little energy of words be different if it were coming out of someone else's mouth? Whose mouth? Can it be more or less true because of who said it? Can it be more interesting or mundane? Play with the string of words. Create a new context. Tell a story that isn't true in its event, but might be true by its offering. Expand. Make more sentences to follow it.

_____

_____

_____

_____

_____

_____

_____

_____

_____

Now, go to the reading—to meditating on words, but keep in mind there's a little bit more writing at the end of this entry . . .

24 | listen

He told them another parable: "The kingdom of heaven is like a mustard seed,
which a man took and planted in his field. Though it is the smallest of all
seeds, yet when it grows, it is the largest of garden plants and becomes a tree,
so that the birds come and perch in its branches."

—Matthew 13:31–32

Today's meditation is composed using the same exercise from the previous page—over the course of a few weeks, I listened and recorded. All of these sentences were ones I'd heard, read, or overheard, then tweaked here and there, played with, punched up, gave new contexts. In my journal—alongside my daily reflection and writing—you'd find lists and quick jots of events, sayings, over-hears, anything really, even the mundane—it's all fodder for daily writing. Are you keeping track?

Maybe your life will feel more real when all the pieces of it fit together just right. Like the bass line under notes of treble. There's a music to every day you get up and walk. Notes of grace ring quietly.

Or maybe it's a little different than that: all the words you have get used just right—the best ways they can be used—and you see standing before you a little land of lyrics, a small city of syllables. Where people live, and move, and have their being, and you're looking down on them with wonder. You want to hold their meanings in just the right way.

Most of us will never be great in the world, especially when measured by its standards—where product, stature, and the bottom line are most important. But measures have a way of being changed over time. There is in the world a way of measuring that has less to do with standing up and more to do with being still. Your life is that small seed etched into earth—the horizon is about to change.

Your voice—that unique view of reality, that humble vision—is waiting in you. Even now you're starting to hear what it can say, how it can change everything.

Your voice is always a contract between who you are and the world in which you move—your unpretentious way that few might ever see, your unassuming place in this vast arena.

You're a small grace becoming. A holy anomaly waking up.

Today, try living and being large by thinking and doing small. Try living life one word at a time, one small note at a time. See what songs you begin to hear yourself hum.

It's your voice and your music—this is your song.

Maybe it's possible that everything comes at just the right time. Could this be the right moment at the right time? A perfect storm for you to swim? A happy accident that you should welcome, celebrate, rejoice in?

When will you see that perfect is complete, that perfect is *poemia*? Can you give yourself to words in a way that will help you live? Did you say anything perfect yesterday? Today?

Yes, maybe everything. No, close to nothing.

It doesn't matter—all of it is already whole, and already yours. ✑

And now this one last little piece of the exercise . . .

Rewrite one sentence from today's meditation and try your best to make it as perfect as possible. Get lucky and make it happen right. This time, sprinkle it with your voice and see what happens. Put the right word in the right place right now. Go.

{ exercise 25 }

Again, before you go on to today's reflection, write fresh. Reflect over a time when your perception shifted—when the Kingdom of God got a little larger, when you felt wrong, humbled, mortified. Chances are this story will be uncomfortable, but push through the event or incidents. Maybe you experienced that strange mix of shame and awe, fear and fathom, guilt and grandness. Being awakened is often both upsetting and exhilarating.

Again, don't just record the events—tell the story, relive the story, let it resonate in your being and on the page. Here's a tip on how to make that happen—describe the individuals involved; the scenery. How are things remembered? Is your memory accurate? It's all right to infer things; open up to the possibility of what was happening—what was there—that you might not be able to remember. Again, use words you might not use in everyday speech—give the narrative a flare and finesse by paying specific attention to surroundings, feelings, and sensory details. When you're done, go on to the meditation.

25 | one spring

My daughter once decided to stay with my wife and me during church, opting out of her preschool Sunday morning class. We were reluctant, worried she might get bored or noisy. We were completely wrong.

In our church, we have an open table policy for Communion—our clergy are firm on the idea that "it's God's table, not ours—all are welcome." I know this idea is offensive to many, fascinating to some, and supported by a few, but it's our belief that if someone is hungry for the body of Jesus then maybe no earthly tie or verbal confession should stand in the way of their receiving the meal. After all, every one of us comes to the altar looking for a handout, and anyone who comes gets a handout—the Economy of God is based on charity, not what's earned.

When the time came, our daughter—who was a little more than three years old at the time—followed us up to the rail. She was as reverent as the rest of us—focused on the sacrament it seemed, prayerfully poised, keeping a penitent pace.

We went to kneel and she followed, fitting between us. We folded our hands to pray. She folded her hands to pray. She mimicked all our motions. The priest came to place wafers in our hands. And before I realized what was happening, my daughter reached out and received the Body. She bowed her head as if she'd been praying for years. When the blood came around, she dipped and ate—one fluid motion.

I was stunned at how fast it had all happened, how natural it seemed; I didn't dare interrupt her; she seemed so resolute. Along with the other forgiven pilgrims, we moved back to our pew, content in our tiny transformations, our little renewals.

I wondered about what the sacrament might do to my little girl—had she changed? After all, the body and blood are designed to change us, revise us, make us new. Is there an age limit? A state of mind that one must achieve before the elements can alter us?

Maybe the sacrament is so radically real and transformative that she was made whole right in front of us. And maybe she did it with the best intentions, for the right reasons—absent pretense, spectacle, vacillation, or worrying about what others might think.

There she was, my daughter lined up along with our whole community of broken believers—a wine soaked wafer, a respectful smile—coming to Christ for the very first time. Sure she might have been doing it just following our lead, and I don't think she understood the significance of it on an intellectual level. But I'd like to find one person that fully gets what goes on in any of the sacramental traditions. It's a sin to mistake our informed best guesses for unshakable certainties.

Maybe her understanding was unadorned, essential, completely clean—*blessed are the pure in heart, for they shall see God.* She closed her little eyes and breathed. It was a holy moment—new acceptance. It's a kind of holiness I've rarely witnessed, only when I'm bathed in the grace of silence, when my life is being revised toward the peace of God—the closest I come to communion without the body and blood of Christ being taken in.

Detractors will be able to see only theology here—they'll balk at what they think is a lack of respect, or determine to keep Christ's kingdom small, elite, and guarded by way of ritualistic practice; they might even say their position is for the sake of unity, continuity, or purity. Some might even call their position God's will for all people. That lack's imagination. The sanctimonious should consider that my daughter—by her own aspiration—came just as Jesus asked us to: as a child—her imagination capable of containing the complexity of God and the simplicity of restitution. God was offered and she stepped forward.

That's the divine streak within us—a great hope locked into the blessed elements. A provision for all of us, even smallest daughters. A shift in the bedrock of a little girl's heart and mind.

God is inviting you into some holy life—will you wander with me, with her, with the rest of us? ᴄᴏ

26 | images

Then his father, Zechariah, was filled with the Holy Spirit and gave this prophecy:

"Praise the Lord, the God of Israel,
because he has visited and redeemed his people.
He has sent us a mighty Savior
from the royal line of his servant David,
just as he promised
through his holy prophets long ago.
Now we will be saved from our enemies
and from all who hate us.
He has been merciful to our ancestors
by remembering his sacred covenant—
the covenant he swore with an oath
to our ancestor Abraham.
We have been rescued from our enemies
so we can serve God without fear,
in holiness and righteousness
for as long as we live.

"And you, my little son,
will be called the prophet of the Most High,
because you will prepare the way for the Lord.
You will tell his people how to find salvation
through forgiveness of their sins.
Because of God's tender mercy,
the morning light from heaven is about to break upon us,
to give light to those who sit in darkness and in the shadow of death,
and to guide us to the path of peace."

—LUKE 1:67–79 NLT

This could be a moment when peace surpasses all understanding. What are you doing here every morning? Why did you show up today? What's this waiting on the Lord? It's not just happening here—believers everywhere are doing this same thing—penitently waiting, entreating, making. You aren't alone. Whether it's known or unknown—acknowledged or unacknowledged—we're all encountering God.

Breath. Prayer. Peace. All of these can be found on your pages. All come forth from this quiet. Images emerge from the ether in us. These are deeply symbolic, and have profound implications in our personal identities. Close your eyes and focus. What appears in your mind? Go on, do it . . .

What image—what small picture—just now came into your mind when you read that last sentence? Significant, no doubt. See it clearer now? Make a note to yourself here:

We're all together in this worship: in joy and lament; in beauty and agony—all of us directly addressing the Maker of All Things. Maybe right now it's happening next door—your neighbors on their knees, praying silently or passing beads, keeping their quiet faith.

We're made with intention—shaped from the dust by the breath of our Creator. Pearls pounded out, smoothed, and brought into the world.

We're made with God's words—poems walking and upright. We create from beauty and awe, from grief and ignorance. What we know and don't know matter equally. We can make as God made.

We must become part of the poem of Christ by living past our experience and into some greater imagination for reconciliation and peace. We cannot let our hearts be troubled; we cannot be afraid. Christ has left with us a bountiful, surpassing peace (John 14:27).

So let this be our prayer together today. Pray it aloud:

Creator, silence my voice and bring forth your own in me. Slowly our pages fill with words, and we are filled also. Let our words be yours, and let us begin our days with them. May they bring peace and hope, faith and love. Let it be your language that lives in, through, and with us. May your name be always on our lips.

It's simple: your voice *here*. Because your words *matter*.

Your voice is bringing about some great change. And God's listening—living in and through your jots and scribbles, giving way to wonder.

And God is giving you the right words.

True poetry is saying exactly. And having the humility to create is necessary to say at all. So this thing you're doing—this art, this life—is a trajectory toward *becoming*. Beginning and ending in what God is making, and what you're helping God make right here.

By our attention, we become God's own poem; by God's attention, our world becomes a poem. So bear yourself to this page—wait and be patient.

Ask and you will receive. Knock and the door will open to you. ᶜᵔᵔ

{ exercise 26 }

Your mind can make some pretty strange associations. But those associations have their roots in the truth of your life and sensory experience, so they're natural occurrences, not simply obscure relatives.

Take a look at that little note you made a few moments ago, the one about the first image that comes to your mind. What is that image *doing* in your head. Why that one? Why not something else? Answer those questions below. Take your best guess. Or if you didn't have an image before, seek one right now. Close your eyes again—what picture appears? Be sure to come up with something. You're going to need it.

_____

_____

_____

_____

_____

_____

_____

Now go ahead and zoom in on that image and begin describing it below. Use fifteen sentences—no more, no less—that explore the sensory aspects of the image. How are you experiencing the thing? What details come forward via your interactions with this object? Describe, describe, describe. Use similes where possible. Get as close to a complete description of the object as you can.

Think hard. There's most certainly a memory attached to this image. What is it? Write its narrative below. Again, ten sentences. If you can't think of a memory, make one up. It isn't wrong to construct something unreal for the purposes of telling the world what's true.

---

27 | what words do

*After John was put in prison, Jesus went into Galilee, proclaiming
the good news of God. "The time has come," he said. "The kingdom of God
is near. Repent and believe the good news!"*

—MARK 1:14–15

Maybe our task as believers interested in bringing what's *at-hand* into the immediate moment should be to treat the Kingdom as something arrived, rather than something that will only come after we die, something that waits beyond this life. Awaken, open, reveal, unveil. If the Kingdom of God is within, then we don't have to wait for Heaven—it's already here, come near, and making its place among us.

Christ says that when two or more are gathered he is there. And it's interesting that language only begins living when two or more are gathered—two friends or lovers, a speaker and audience, a book and a reader, writer and page.

The Kingdom of God is not an isolated empire concerned with borders and bloodlines but an open communion offered to all. Not one, but many.

If you're of the school of thought that says our words matter little, then consider the tower built at Babel—*nothing they plan to do will be impossible . . .*—and the languages scattered across the world. Or, in the wild reversal of those events—in a complete renewing of language—the descent of God's Spirit in Pentecost, where every tongue is a revelatory instrument for God to all people, beginnings borne among us, a creative communication.

From Babel to Pentecost, a whole rearrangement of worlds and laws and governance: chaos and confusion altered to creation and clarity. This is the tradition in which you play a part—your presence means something: God is a God of words, and those words create. They made you, and by them you can make as well.

So there's hope in the language we offer one another here in this world that's not contingent on other worlds to come. We can offer hope to one another right now, this side of eternity. Those words become poetry when we offer them with intention. These are benedictions.

That being said, if poetry does one thing—or should do one thing—it binds us together in common humanity. Whether you write to explain what and who you are, or you write for an audience, ultimately writing belongs to some larger body than your own.

It's reaching outward by moving inward. It's going the wide road to others by walking the narrow road inside. If you didn't want to reach outside the walls of your own mind and experience, there would be no need for you to use words at all. You use words every day. You have an ache for communion.

When we make with our words, we reach outward, move against ourselves and our privacies, our best kept secrets, our long and little lives. If it weren't true, why would there be a need for articulation at all, why not live with such complete apathy toward adding your vision to the world? Why speak—even a little?

We want an experience *together*. And poetry can be that act of community we crave. So the question now becomes something closer to how can we come together and make something come alive, shine with meaning, shimmer in the radiant light of the world?

Your words are great—those ones on your lips right now. They belong to something else—a larger body, a great cloud of witnesses, allegiance to a Creator that allows us to create. These words announce the new Economy, here and soon coming. ⌒

{ exercise 27 }

Examine the image—that picture that appeared in your mind—from yesterday's exercise and answer the following questions about it below . . .

How is this image a symbol in the context of what I currently know and experience? Is there—in its essence—evidence that it was made intentionally? Yes, I know it's cryptic and a bit weird.

_____

_____

_____

_____

What are some pieces of your vocabulary that you might use to describe the object to someone else—think literally _and_ figuratively. Maybe list all the words appearing in your mind right now—just write them out.

_____

_____

_____

_____

This one will take some imagination: Talk to the image and tell it how and why you are made in the image of your Creator. Speak in a way that you imagine it might speak, in a way it might understand. Don't whine or groan about it, just try it—it's okay if it's strange.

_____

_____

_____

_____

_____

_____

What might the image say back to you? What does completeness mean to you now that you've spoken with this image, named it, opened it, really added it to you?

_____

_____

_____

_____

_____

_____

28 | this is not goodbye

For we are God's poemia, *created in Jesus Christ to do **good works**, which God prepared in advance for us to do.*

—EPHESIANS 2:10

Where are you going today?

There's a road you've been following your whole life—a cut carved for you, for your days of wandering, seeking, seeing. There's nothing more or less beautiful than its singular direction.

It's what you're becoming. And now you see it a little more clearly. Not because of something you read, but by way of something you wrote.

Your voice here.

Today's the day for a quiet revolution. A full silence. A day for you to be awake and see the world.

You woke up today. And that's a gift. How will you ever repay that?

You can start by offering. Start by walking into the world and seeing it clearly. Or at least trying to.

This is the new Economy of God: completeness. It's the new perfection. It's the palace within you made of words.

That's poetry: that Economy spilling over, colliding with ordinary language—the moment when you realize that you're an inimitable word spoken from the mouth of God, the Maker.

God's doing a new thing *right now, right here*. There are good works for you to make manifest in this lifetime, in this world, in this very second. On these papers, with that pencil, through that pen. You're looking at the world around you and God is looking back—from those pages, through that window, from the table top—immanent, alive, so near. Intimate as air.

Think of this space for a moment. You don't know who came before you, or who will come after. You know so little about where you are—the secret conversations, the laughter, the grief—the very present but unknown facts of the space where you're living. There's a whole history here, a whole memory to which you're forever bound.

Never forget that this is a road you've been walking, and people have been seeing your steps. Never forget there's a road you're on, and that a cloud of witnesses surrounds you. Never forget there's a road ahead, and it's a road we'll walk together. This is happening as you read these words. As you write your words.

This space will never be perfect—and it can never be fully known—but we can begin to open our attentions to its potential to give us life by way of exploration. We must learn about grace not from what's perfect but what's imperfect. Grace needs imperfection far more than flawlessness.

Nothing you make, are, or do will ever be perfect. And that's the beautiful thing. What better way to spend your life than to try and revise yourself, your world, your soul into something closer to God?

The words you've written this month, the words you'll write after it, are part of your poem. A language only you can say with your mouth and your words, from a hand outstretched that only you can open.

Here it is again: the small proof of what you are—your moments clear, your life in this place, your understanding of these things.

So go today, walk out, and live the words of peace that you're becoming. Remember that, like you, your offerings are fearfully and wonderfully made.

What can you offer today that will reorder everything toward God coming into the world? Toward the Word made Flesh?

Perhaps a hello and goodbye in every word you make. Perhaps everything you aren't and everything you are in one slight saying. Perhaps a voice you're just now beginning to hear. Perhaps nothing more than some syllables ringing infinitely away from this solitary, short-lived space. ᔐ

{ exercise 28 }

This is it. Your last solo exercise in the book. Take a second to flip through the book if you choose, to see how far you've come. Pretty great stuff, right? And because you've been writing this whole time—and doing so creatively—you now have a trail. You can see, step by step, the path you've taken to get to this moment here. That's not just realization, but epiphany.

Go through the week's exercises—in all their weirdness—and see what comes up. Is there a relationship between the scribbles you've made and the life that you live, the people that you meet, and the world that you record?

So here's our last exercise: Write a poem making an object you've observed over the course of the week a vehicle for some kind of redemption between you and another individual. What's your object? Think about how this object might be an avenue to realization, grace, and awakening. Think about it symbolically, metaphorically. I know, it's tough. Write it. Write about it.

_____

_____

Choose one of the following as the basis for the poem. Pick whichever one you feel will give you the most juice, the most challenge, or the one you think you might need to do, however hard that may be . . .

> Write a poem where you're *asking* for guidance.
> Write a poem where you're *giving* guidance.
> Write a poem where you're *asking* for forgiveness.
> Write a poem where you're *giving* forgiveness.

It would be strange and silly to be direct in this exercise, so you must do one of the above indirectly, using all your accumulated talents for sensing out the meanings under meaning, the beings under being. Never in the poem are you allowed to directly ask for whichever you chose from the options above. And, as usual, no rhyming here. Oh, and to add a little flavor, be sure that one of those names of God makes it into the poem.

And don't forget to have fun . . .

_____

_____

_____

_____

_____

_____

_____

_____

_____

_____

community building

In the following sections you'll find materials that you can use if you're using this book as more than just as personal devotional guide. Many of you might be using this book with a friend, or as part of a large-group study (Bible/Sunday school class, writing workshop, classroom textbook, retreat guide), or in any other situation where you might be working individually but coming together with others to discuss your week's entries, your jots, and the other materials found within these pages.

When you come together (breaking off in small groups of 8–10 if needed), set aside sixty to ninety minutes to do at least two (you probably won't be able to do all three unless you have at least two hours) of the following activities.

1. *Group Discussion*: These reflective questions often ask for personal reactions, but also cover ideas about poetry, faith, and writing. It would be a good idea for the group's leader to read through the discussion questions before facilitating the group, so that he or she has a good idea of where the discussion might lead and might choose the questions that would be best for the group as a whole. Allow the conversation to be open and honest. If silence occurs, allow it; become comfortable with one another in quiet. If no one answers in a reasonable amount of time, feel free to move on. Also, be open to following trails away from the program— you never know where they might lead.

2. *Workshop*: This activity asks participants to *share their writing* from over the course of the week. This is intimidating for some, but the group should be comforted by the fact they're wandering the wilderness together, and that sharing writing— which in this case is distinctly personal—is a great way to build community, and quickly. Creativity requires vulnerability right from the start.

    A good workshop should always begin with the person reading his or her piece through aloud. After the reading, the author should be *completely silent* and listen.

This is a hard but useful practice, since the author will get to hear the group experience the piece on their own terms, rather than the author telling the group how they'd hoped the group might experience it. In an ideal world, the reader should take nothing personally—remember, people aren't reacting to you but the poem, which has its own life that must be shaped. The author should also take notes about what the group says and consider them later.

After the poem is read, someone from the group should try to summarize it in one or two sentences so that the group can discern how it works as a whole. For example: "This is a poem where the speaker is ruminating on an old chair found in his parents' house. The chair itself is a symbol of lost innocence because . . ." After the poem has been summarized, the group should respond with *constructive feedback*—suggestions on the poem's weak spots, like the line breaks, diction, images, etc., and praise of the poem's strong points. The reactions shouldn't be excessively personal. It doesn't help the author of the poem to know that chair symbolism in the poem reminded you of your dead relative's chair, but it would help the author to know that the symbol is useful and clearly serves to anchor the poem in some vivid idea. The group should be sensitive to the personal nature of sharing a piece and respond to it accordingly—what's working or not working, what does the poem say to the world, and how does it say what it's saying. If the group gets stuck, they can refer to the Revision Checklist to zero in on smaller pieces of the poem. Feel free to ask one another questions or read pieces of the poem aloud again if needed.

Try to make time for each person to share a poem. It's important that everyone try and share a piece over the course of your time together. Some people will be more eager to participate than others. No one should be forced to share their work, but it should be understood that workshopping a piece is valuable for building a cohesive group identity and trust between group members—patience and compassion will go a long way to helping those with trepidation. Those who are hesitant should challenge themselves to open up and make an offering to the group—no hiding that light under a bushel!

3. *Writing Exercises*: There are four large-group writing exercises, one for each meeting of your group over the twenty-eight days. Each one should have a solid thirty minutes to be conducted, so that people have freedom to think and write. Be sure that the group leader has fully read and understands the exercise—that way he or she can answer questions, shape the exercise if needed, and help guide others in the group; he or she should ignore the requests for surprise so that the

group might be properly guided. If the group gets stuck, it's up to the leader to reframe the exercise.

Of course, you can do these exercises solo if you're doing the book on your own. Consider them four bonus cuts! Move through each exercise by number giving a few minutes for each portion; follow the directions and don't go looking ahead—some of the exercises function on surprises. Once the group leader who is conducting the exercise sees pens and pencils slowing down—stopping—he or she can move on to the next portion of the exercise. There should be a respectful silence in the room, as hard as that might be at times. You also might want to consider workshopping the piece written during the exercise time, directly after the exercise time is finished. Lastly, remember that nothing great might come from your exercises; often exercises are most helpful in teaching you how your mind works, or helping you find a trail to begin following. Keep your expectations for your writing low.

The following pieces are integral to community building through the act of writing. Remember, writing isn't a static process, but a living one based on how we interact with one another and the world; so this—discussion, creating together, and sharing our creations—is a natural course of action for people yearning for deeper community.

Get going!   ◞

five rules for believing writers

For those both innocent and experienced in the ways of writing, here are some rules for your times of daily practice. Of course, when it comes to making art—to making manifest that still, small voice inside you—rules are more like strong suggestions, nothing hard and fast, so there's no need to be stringent about them. It will also do some good to notice that these "rules to write by" are also good rules to live by. Let these ideas govern your time . . .

1. trust yourself . . .

Even if you don't know what you're doing, learning to rely on your gut in writing will rarely steer you wrong. **It's important to remember that your life *is* a poem. And poems that we make on paper are just extensions of our living poetry.** As Ephesians 2:10 says, you are God's workmanship—God's *poemia*—and that's reason enough to engage this process with confidence. Workmanship implies time, energy, and progression, so it's best to just go with what comes out while you write, even if it seems to make little sense, appears upsetting, strange, gushing, or sentimental. Those things are just your gut talking, so you should probably listen up! Think of it as refinement—allow yourself into the process and the strange negotiation that is *becoming*.

2. get away from measuring . . .

To write well, you must get rid of expectations and standards. **Let come what offers itself; put down everything that emerges from you without regard for quality.** Never erase or eradicate, simply strike through things you don't think you want. Where you are and what you're doing is just right—nothing more or less is needed; you don't have to humble or exalt yourself, cower or roar: just be. This world might have told you otherwise, but things are different now. In writing—while you're creating—there are no gaps, errors, or needless sidetracks. Everything you write could be revised to something more lovely later. Like our faith, our writing is never what it will be when it first presents itself. Put away your high standards and welcome what comes. Its transformation—and yours—will come soon enough.

3. remember that what you create is something close to holy . . .

It's true, though you might not believe it. No matter how flat, ugly, or bizarre, what you're making in your times of solitude is complete. **Even if it doesn't seem complete in what it *says*, it is so in what it *is*. When you create, you reflect the Creator in the opening of Genesis, and you should look down on your little creation and say it's "*good*."** Worry about the beauty of the thing later, since beauty and holiness are two different animals, and often unrelated.

4. practice silence . . .

When you're here, be here. No screens of any kind—turn off the phone, TV, or computer. You might ask: *what if I write on a computer?* For this month, I'd like you to try the pencil and page. If you're reading this as an e-book, disable the internet capability and commit to hand writing your words on an actual paper page—this will help you focus and move slow. Write in the space provided here or in your personal journal. Paper is silent and simple; computers are filled and connected to all kinds of noise—the bellowing chaos of the news and politics, the blabbering of social media, and the soft, tempting glow of every kind of distraction. **Be content—just for a short time—to sit unwired, unbothered, in the quiet of your home. Be still and enjoy it.** Do as Christ urges in Luke 12 and consider the lilies—be present, pay attention—don't cultivate concern but focus.

5. practice slowness . . .

Find that place—that physical location—in your daily routine that makes you feel at peace in your life and do your meditation and exercise there if feasible. At home, in the break room at work, in the calm of a cluttered coffee shop—wherever you feel comfortable and can work undistracted. Clear a way for yourself—look outside, calculate, meditate, mull. Chances are you already have a place in mind and that place slows you down, blocks out the speed of the world, or helps you focus; a place that allows you to sit unnoticed. **Be intentional about your time and try to set some aside to write and create at the same time every day.** I suggest the morning, when you and the day are both new again. Contemplate, focus, deliberate—take your time and make it sacred again. Designate a space as holy, maybe even to the point where you only utilize that space for writing, for creation and communion.

week 1

discussion questions

1. Do you find the poem "Your Days Are Waiting" easy or hard to understand? What makes it so? What insights about the poem can you provide to the rest of the group that might be helpful, key others in? Be specific—what words, phrases, lines, or images give you the impression that you have?

2. What are some things that you'd like to *etch* in yourself—your moons, leaves, and stars? What are the things about your life that you might like to capture in your writing? What is inside your mind that waits to slip away?

3. Who comes to mind when you read a poem like "Your Days Are Waiting"? Is there a person that you think might like this poem, or benefit from it? Why? What does this poem offer to a reader?

4. What is the hardest part about the way human beings remember their lives? Why is our memory so incomplete, so easily misunderstood, misinterpreted, or fleeting? Is there a memory you have that you wish you didn't? Or one that you wish was more full?

5. Describe your most vivid early memory to the group. Why do you think you remember this event or circumstance? Why is this significant to you?

6. Discuss your experiences in poetry with the rest of the group. What do you like and dislike about poetry? Why? What experiences have shaped this opinion?

7. What value does poetry offer people? Why write it, read it, support it, or celebrate it? What does poetry's presence in your world (or lack thereof!) do? If poetry isn't present in your life, do you think it could offer you something that you don't currently have?

8. How do you think writing and reading poetry might deepen your belief system? How might it help you and your community reimagine faith and the way you act out your faith in the world? What can writing actually *do* for Christ followers and the way they interact with God's created people?

9. Has this week of writing been easy or hard for you? Why do you think that is? What might make it easier? Are there any best practices that you've used this week that you can share that might help others?

10. How are memory and the Christian life related? What are some functions of memory—both personal and collective—for believers? And how are they both related to language? To poetry? To shaping our communities?

workshop

Begin by summarizing the poem read aloud in one or two sentences so that all the workshoppers are operating from the same context. Then move through the questions that follow.

1. How is this poem about "awakening"?

2. What are some of the poem's strongest elements?

3. What are some of the poem's weakest elements?

4. How might the author go about revising? Be sure to give practical advice. If you're struggling for ideas on what to revise, take a look at the Revision Checklist for some help.

exercise: line, align

For this exercise, you'll be writing some lines and forming them into a small poem.

1. Begin by imagining an object you'd find in your backyard—it can be anything, organic or synthetic.

2. Write a line that is eight words long about the object—and only eight words. No going over or under!

3. Skip a line on the page and rewrite the line, this time removing two words and adding a new one.

4. Now, write a line that responds to what you wrote in the previous step—a companion line—making the singular line a couplet. It also should be only eight words.

5. Immediately revise the line you just made, again taking out two words and replacing it with one.

6. Repeat steps 2–5 until your time is up—don't stop writing if possible. Just keep going forward until the group leader tells you to stop.

Once the time is up, take a moment to share your answers aloud. Don't be shy—everyone is on an even playing field. What you've just written is probably malformed junk, but you never know what might come from it. ⌒

week 2

discussion questions

1. What is the significance of "believing in ghosts" in the poem "Ghost Story"? How does the idea of ghost stories serve to unify the poem?

2. Discuss the line "As if you cupped your hands to drink—water leaking slow around the knuckles." What does the image have to do with the poem? With love? With memory?

3. Why do you think first kisses are so important to our personal development? Why is there such significance placed upon them? Is it possible that the act of kissing might help us to understand God in a unique way? Why or why not? Is the act of kissing a spiritual act? Why or why not?

4. When you were writing this week, did any strange memories come forward? Ones you forgot about? Take some time to share a couple of memories with the group.

5. What are some smells that trigger your strongest memories? Can you recall a time when a smell brought a memory forward in a potent way?

6. What might faith, imagination, and language have to do with one another? What's the nature of their relationship, especially for creative people?

7. What do you feel is the value of writing in your life, your community, and the larger context of where you live? What do you hope your practice of writing might accomplish? As an individual, as a group? What can it make you see?

8. What has what you've been working on in this daily program—your daily writing— taught you about the way you think, comprehend, or make connections? What pieces of your puzzle seem to be coming together? What narratives seem to be telling and retelling themselves?

9. What is it about a good metaphor that opens our hearts and minds to the larger world? Why do you think we respond so strongly to a good metaphor, to a good story?

10. What are some ways that daily devotional practice rooted in playing with words might benefit you spiritually? How might it benefit the world around you, the people in your life?

workshop

Begin by summarizing the poem read aloud in one or two sentences so that all the workshoppers are operating from the same context. Then move through the questions that follow.

1. How is this poem about human connectedness? What does this poem have to say about the way people interact with one another and the divine?

2. What are some of the poem's strongest elements?

3. What are some of the poem's weakest elements?

4. How might the author go about revising? Be sure to give practical advice. If you're struggling for ideas on what to revise, take a look at the Revision Checklist for some help.

exercise: to whom it may concern . . .

For this exercise, you'll be writing a small letter, an epistolary poem. We'll be writing down some names, ideas, and—finally—some lines of poetry. I'm going to be providing examples below, but don't look at them unless you need to or get stuck.

1. Begin by drawing a line vertically down the center of the top half your paper.

2. Make one half *Column A* and the other *Column B*.

3. Now, in *Column* A, make a list of six living people—no one is off limits.

4. In *Column B* make a list of six characters from the Bible—the first six that pop into your head (you can't write down Jesus). They should be characters whose biographies you know a little about, whose stories you can recall.

A	B
Charles Manson	Elijah
Brad (friend)	Adam
Paul Anka	Eve
Amy (sister)	Ruth
Anthony (cousin)	Paul
Margaret Thatcher	Peter

5. Now, you're going to write three quick letters—epistles—between five and ten sentences long.

6. In each letter, you should . . .

   a. Tell a story that comes to mind when you think of that individual.
   b. Admit or confess something.
   c. Finish the letter with an open-ended question.

7. Now, for each epistle, you'll choose (and do so quickly—not too much thinking!) one individual from the column stated below.

8. Here's the order . . .

   a. Letter 1 should be from *A* to *B* *OR* from *B* to *A*.
   b. Letter 2 should be from *A* to *you* *OR* from *you* to *A*.
   c. Letter 3 should be from *B* to *you* *OR* *you* to *B*.

Take your time writing, and be sure to think about the narratives of the lives of these individuals you've chosen. Look for opportunities to give or receive advice, use quotes or colloquialism from the individual's life, or use significant or symbolic narrative details. Remember that this exercise might turn out some strange results, but there's nothing wrong with that—all things in you are working toward some greater good.

I'm providing an example of this exercise below so that you might see how this exercise works and that not all of the results of these exercises reap great rewards, but help us to think in ways we haven't before.

To Charles Manson,

Yesterday I was walking down the street and saw a bearded hobo holding a sign saying *The End is Near* and I thought to myself *Well, I better get home and see my wife and kids*. I'm writing this now because this guy looked just like you—beard, beady eyes, and that intense, terrible glare—though he had no symbols on his forehead.

After thinking about the sign, I decided that I don't always treat people how I should, especially the ones I really love—I want to fix that. I'm hoping that you understand this, what with all your time to think.

I wonder, are there *any* people that you've loved? Ever? And what do those people that you love know about you that we don't? Would you resolve to do it over? To never command those young, sick children?

Thanks,
Dave

Again, keep pushing forward—often the strangest thing ends up being the most fruitful. ⌒

week 3

discussion questions

1. What's the strangest thing that's happened to you this week? Spend some time swapping stories from the past seven days of activity—good, bad, ugly; fun, crumby, mundane.

2. Much of the Bible is very concerned with language. Why do you think language is important to God? What's sacred about our words and the way we use them? Why is God a God of words? Can you give an uncommon example from scripture?

3. What is the hardest part about writing every day? What have you been learning about spiritual discipline, your own spiritual gifts, and the creative nature of God?

4. How have you gotten better at noticing small things in your daily experience? Is there value in the world as humans have shaped it? Is there anything holy about what we make? Why?

5. What do the lines "The sun comes forward—an orchestrated prayer— / after snow rehearses what it will mean to become water" from "Was Blind" mean to you? Or how about "We're all meeting under a banner that knows / we've been loving one another since birth?"

6. What's the significance of the spider in "Was Blind"? What does the image of it crawling away represent?

7. What's the significance of the line breaks in "Was Blind"? Why do you think the lines are broken the way they are? How could they be broken differently? What would a revision of the line breaks do to the poem?

8. Discuss a connection you've made with an animal. What's it like? Why is it significant? What does our connection to the natural world say about the nature of God's creative character, the way God made the world?

9. Can you think back to something that seemed insignificant at the time but is now realized as a turning point in your life? How do the small actions in your life open to the larger plan that God has for your life?

10. What has God gifted you with—a skill, ability, or anything else—that could be an instrument for radical change toward peace, compassion, reconciliation, faith, hope, and love in our world?

workshop

Begin by summarizing the poem read aloud in one or two sentences so that all the workshoppers are operating from the same context. Then move through the questions that follow.

1. How does this poem deal with the sacredness of the small, the human-made, or the seemingly inconsequential detail?

2. What are some of the poem's strongest elements?

3. What are some of the poem's weakest elements?

4. How might the author go about revising? Be sure to give practical advice. If you're struggling for ideas on what to revise, take a look at the Revision Checklist for some help.

exercise: five little haikus

For this exercise, you're going to write five little poems—haikus, actually. Haikus are a Japanese form of poetry that underscores the beauty, elegance, and mystery of the natural world and an individual's place within it. Haiku is meditative and rich—capturing a vivid moment on the cusp of awakening—even though its only a seventeen syllable poem.

Those seventeen syllables are spread out over three lines and should keenly observe the world, but not necessarily arrive at any conclusion about it. If you're stuck, go ahead and check out the examples below. They were written right on the spot—one while looking out the window, one while sitting outside. They aren't the best haikus ever written, but they'll work for now. Writing a haiku is a quick and simple way to practice your skills of observation and language brevity, so consider writing one haiku per day from this day forward!

Today, you'll be writing five haikus—a total of fifteen lines. Each line should adhere to a strict syllable count, like this . . .

Form	Example A	Example B
five syllables	Still trees, morning blue—	Stalks bending, cold air.
seven syllables	say the grace you know by heart.	Winter carving out its way.
five syllables	Mist from grass, blue jays	Dancing flakes, light fades.

1. Begin this exercise by going outside if that's feasible. If not, go find some windows and take a look outside together.

2. Spend a few minutes still, silent watching—just looking, observing. Do your best to allow the world around you to forget that you're there, watching.

3. Zero in on a couple of objects, actions, feelings, sensory details and begin to sketch out the world around you in words. As usual, worry little about quality and focus on the moment, the awakening, to the actions and essences before you.

Remember, your presence in that place at that precise time changes everything. What things are waiting to reveal themselves to you?

week 4

discussion questions

1. How do you plan to continue moving forward now that this intensive study is winding down? What are some ways you might cultivate imagination in your devotional practice from here on out?

2. How have you and your beliefs changed or shifted over the course of this month? What's been made new in you? What's stayed the same?

3. How can your community be reimagined to be a more gracious, loving group of people living to bring about the Economy of God in some tangible ways, however small? What are some points of improvement? What are you already doing well? How can creativity enrich your community, and the community around you? How could it prompt you to take bold steps? What might those steps be?

4. Go back to Day 23—"Basic Math"—and discuss some of the questions found there. What's the purpose of asking such questions? What are some of your answers to them? How can what you've done here better help you love your neighbors and your enemies?

5. What's been your favorite part about this study? Your least favorite part? Why?

6. Are your daily writings—your images, descriptions, observations, scribbles—good or bad? Why? What makes them so? What will your jots in this book amount to? Why are they both important and unimportant?

7. What's the significance of the image of the tree in "To Mark the Place?" What do you see this poem being about?

8. All the poems in this book mention stars. Why do you think stars are a significant image to a book like this? To the poems themselves? How might they be an apt metaphor for our lives and what our lives represent?

9. How is what you've been doing over the past few weeks an act of communal/collective remembering, or memory making? Is what you've done here important to God? Why or why not? How does "To Mark the Place" commemorate that idea?

10. Where do the allusions in stanza 7 of "To Mark the Place" come from? What does it mean for "anathema" become "incantation"?

workshop

Begin by summarizing the poem read aloud in one or two sentences so that all the workshoppers are operating from the same context. Then move through the questions that follow.

1. How is this poem about the opening of the Kingdom of God, to the speaker, to the world?

2. What are some of the poem's strongest elements?

3. What are some of the poem's weakest elements?

4. How might the author go about revising? Be sure to give practical advice. If you're struggling for ideas on what to revise, take a look at the Revision Checklist for some help.

exercise: psalm writing exercise

Go outside and complete the exercise below. It's important—for the sake of the gut reaction—that you don't read ahead but take each statement as it comes. Good luck!

1. Write five sentences—each one describing what's around you, using one of the five senses (see, taste, touch, smell, hear).

2. Write a *simile* (comparison using *like* or *as*) connecting an emotion to a natural object that you see—don't write down the first emotion that comes to mind; write down the third.

3. Steal a line or two from one of the poems in this book—which poem seems to connect strongly with how you feel, what you think, or what you see? Choose whichever lines you'd like.

4. Make a statement that describes the beauty that you see.

5. Make a statement that describes the ugliness you see.

6. Write three sentences about what *hunger* means.

7. Write three sentences about what *thirst* means.

8. Pick up a *natural* object from the ground and describe it in detail using the same sensory language you did above.

9. Tell how that object represents what you consider to be your childhood home. How does it represent the emotional climate of your home? How does it represent your parents? Positively or negatively. At least five sentences . . .

10. Tell how that object represents some aspect of human sensuality. At least three sentences . . .

11. Tell how that object represents "majesty." At least three sentences . . .

12. Now that you have all these 'notes,' go about composing a poem.

13. Go back inside and sit down. Take the best of what you've written—the lines that speak to you! The poem should be at least sixteen lines and written in couplets—two line stanzas.

14. Use at least three of the following words (in any form) in the poem you're writing. Work these words in as you write! Keep in mind that many of these words have multiple uses as different parts of speech or by definition . . .

Grave	Stake	Habit
Stand	Shift	Form
Clear	Quake	Hammer
Dive	Blow	Creep
Cut	Break	Clear
Drive	Cleavage	Gravity
Dust	Fracture	Fair
Flake	Luster	Grow
Beat	Streak	Braid

Tinker with this poem for a little while, then come together as a group and share the psalms you've written. Does the piece feel like a psalm? Why or why not? What are some of the trappings of the biblical psalms that you see in the poem you've just written?

revision checklist

You might wonder what to do when you've finished writing a poem, but the poem doesn't feel quite "done." You must revise. Revision is where the actual writing starts; it's where you prune, shape, and hone the piece into something more than just an exercise for your own consumption or personal growth. Revision is where poems come to life and move past your journal.

Some people rewrite poems over and over until they feel just right. Almost no poems come ready-made, needing little revision—so get used to the idea that if you'd like to make something worth reading, you're going to have to put in more time. Revising a poem is like looking inside a music box at the tiny engine that makes the wonderful song—there are many considerations and motions. Each little piece has its own function, its own purpose. And when the pieces are whirring just right—all together—a lovely sound materializes.

Below is a checklist that will walk you through some of the moving parts of a poem. I use this checklist whenever I get stuck, or feel something is missing. Heck, sometimes I use it systematically when I'm finished with a poem so that I can see what might need to be tweaked, changed, or shifted. Use it as you wish!

After providing a one to two sentence summary of the poem, ask the following questions . . .

1. Is the poem . . .

    a. *lyrical* (A brief subjective poem strongly marked by imagination, melody, and emotion, and creating a single unified impression)?

    b. *narrative* (A poem that tells a story)?

    c. *dramatic* (A poem that contains natural or unnatural dialogue, monologue, vigorous diction, blank verse, or stressing of a tense situation or emotional conflict)?

2. Bottom line: How does the poem function? Is the poem powerful in its desired function? Give a gut reaction to the poem.

3. How does the poem hit the ear? How does it feel, sonically, inside the mind? Read aloud?

    a. *voice/tone* (Who is speaking? To whom? What is the speaker's tone? What is revealed about the speaker's ideology?)

    b. *sound* (How does sound modify the poem's quality and clarity? Do sounds recur? How does sound contribute to the poem's music? Are rhyme, assonance, consonance, onomatopoeia employed to expand the poem sonically?)

    c. *diction/syntax* (Are words concrete or abstract? Suggestive or straightforward? Mono- or polysyllabic? Any repetition? Does the syntactical consistency foster monotony? Are words used/spelled correctly? Is the grammar correct? Would the author be embarrassed if he/she said the poem was finished?)

4. Form—What is the form of the poem? Does the poem adhere to any kind of pattern? If the form is preexisting, how carefully are the rules followed? How do deviations from the form contribute to or detract from the poem's desired quality?

5. Images—Does the poem employ metaphor, simile, or personification? Is the imagery fresh and exciting? Do the images push the poem forward and make the poem's world larger? Are the images too personal to be understood by others? What feelings do the images evoke?

6. Lines—How do the line breaks serve or hinder the poem? Do they seem natural or forced? Do the line breaks create suspense and tension? Do they underscore something inappropriate or undesired? Are the lines broken in strange places? Do the breaks create interesting or unintended meanings? Do they add to the function of the poem? Are the end stops a kind of grease that keeps the machine oiled and moving smoothly, helping the reader move through the poem with ease?

7. Does the poem require the reader to perform mental gymnastics that are too strenuous, taxing, stressful, or daunting? Is the content worth the investment in the poem? What is the pay-off? Do the poem's shifts have a purpose? Is it too much for one poem? Can the poem be broken into pieces (a series of separate poems) to be more clear or provocative?

8. Are the poem's facts correct? Will this poem make the author or speaker appear ignorant or untrustworthy? If the facts are not correct, does it have a purpose? If you're going to break the rules you must know them first so that you can break them in a meaningful way.

9. Does the poem contain hidden treasures? Functional double-meanings? Engaging variety of language? Driving cadence? Does it bear the author's signature? Does the poem create a lasting relationship with the reader?

10. Can this poem be easily ignored or will people want to share it? If so, why? If not, why? What will the reader remember after they've finished reading the poem? And for how long? ᴄᴏ

coming to poetry: a reflection

I began *reading* poetry because I could never finish novels. I'm not sure this is how many people come to poetry, but it was my route. In high school, I only read a handful of the assigned novels (a mistake I deeply regret now as an adult!) but I read every single poem. When I got to the end of a poem I felt like I had accomplished something, been invited into something—I felt like I'd been given a key.

I liked poetry at that point in my life, but I didn't love it.

I began *writing* poetry because I wanted to impress a girl—maybe this is how most young men come to poetry. I *really* wanted to date her. Poetry—something she liked—seemed a good way to break the ice. I wrote her a terrible poem (I hope to this day she hasn't kept it!) and sent it to her. She read it and loved it; we dated a while.

Still, I liked poetry at that point in my life, but I didn't love it.

I was in college when I began taking poetry seriously—I imagine this is where most people get serious about poetry, if they haven't already or ever do. I realized it wasn't a means to an end—not to make myself feel better about being slower than everyone else, not to help me round the bases. I was taking a writing class for an extracurricular requirement, but I was excited to be there. We were sent home with a packet of poems to read for the next class.

Dead center in the packet was William Stafford's "Traveling Through the Dark"—a brilliant poem about the author's experience finding a dead deer on a narrow road and getting out of his car to move the animal for the good of the order, so that animal might not cause an accident. He soon sees there's more to the situation—that the doe is pregnant and her fawn is still alive inside her. He then makes a tough decision—a decision that echoes through the wilderness all around him.

That's when it happened—that's when my *like* modulated to something else.

My reaction to this poem was bizarrely physical—nothing like it had ever happened to me while I was reading. And though that was my experience, I recognize that I'm probably in a minority. It's okay if people aren't pierced by a poem like I was, but that doesn't negate their value or the reader's ability to glean some wild and beautiful truth from the poem. Or, more likely, you just haven't read the right poem yet.

As I read the Stafford poem's title, I got up to get an apple from the kitchen. By the time I came back to the couch—apple in hand—the deer's secret had been revealed. My breath got a bit short, my neck tensed—I'm not sure why. My heart was pumping a little harder. I felt like I had been punched—the moral imperative, the cruel grief of accidents. All of it made me sit up straight, lean forward with intent. By the end of the poem I was dumbfounded—speechless and still. I sat for quite a while; it was all I could do.

For such a short poem, "Traveling through the Dark" is incredibly varied and complex—the worlds within worlds and the movement between them; the narrowing of the natural world leading to the realization of life, then the broadening of the natural world as it moves outward again; the still, small, peaceful sensibility of intention; and the ethical question at the pith: is it ever right to kill? All packed away with vivid coolness.

As he makes his decision, the speaker says *"I thought hard for all of us . . ."* A gripping clarity—it's the moment in the poem where the speaker in the poem—in this case, William Stafford himself—reaches out beyond himself and hopes one of us might grab his hand, that one of us might join him in witness, in mourning, in a community awake to graces and tragedies of our lives together.

Stafford was thinking hard for me. Stafford was thinking hard for you. And he was thinking about something we probably haven't been thinking about much at all. Shame on us.

Since that moment, I've believed very deeply that poetry's sole purpose is to attach us to one another, and I've allowed that guidance to shape my life—the connection has grown. If a poem isn't reaching out its hand in peace, in reconciliation, in contemplation, in witness, then I get bored and move on from it. I want poems of the bystander trying to make sense of the world. I want poems of rich experience written by women and men unable to turn away from what they must see and what they must say. I want poems that awaken me and call me out of my inertia. If the poem is too detached or too ecstatic, I bristle—they're fallacies of human emotion, in a way. I want the poem that gives life by being true to life.

It's funny that one little poem altered the trajectory of my existence in such a way. After that day, I woke up. I adopted a new way of being—one rooted in daily writing and poetry, one that I haven't left since. For better or worse, all of my decisions have been made with this in mind. And I do my best to go forward every day into the world and see it for what it is, render it in my words. I'm going forward every day with the knowledge that my vocation is to bring people together, to write the story of who I am and the decisions I'm making—of the person I'm becoming.

I'm trying my best to read and write poems that think hard for all of us. I've maybe come close a couple times—a lofty aim, right?

Wish me luck. ∽

works with soul: an interview with *ruminate* magazine

Tell us a little bit about your story, your writing, and your new project, Antler.

First, let me say thanks to *Ruminate* for their interest in my little project, but most of all for making a much-needed space where seekers can come to 'chew on faith, life and art'—I'm glad to have such pleasant ties with what I think is one of the best darn lit mags out there. *Ruminate* is sleek, readable, and challenging in all the right ways!

In my own life, I've been writing seriously for almost a decade, been teaching a little longer, and have always been attracted to poetry, prose, and practices that traverse the strange territory between faith and imagination—I'm interested in how people of faith use their language to open the door to the divine. But I think there's a little more to that ancient practice than entering into the presence of the divinity, and the Christian faith has its own unique revelation for this.

For me, I'm trying to be still long enough for the opposite to happen. Daily contemplation and writing practice, prayer, and peace-making—all things that underscore our humble place in God's world—invite us to that space where the divine's presence already is in this world; I want to awaken to the reality that God's language has come into the very moments in which we're all *being*.

It's very elusive, but worthwhile—it's these practices I want to teach my children and students to engage, and ones that I'm hoping to engage when I sit down to write each morning. Sometimes I come close to something like it, I think, but mostly I just try to.

So, then, where did you first see a real need for imagination and creativity in the religious communities you participated in?

My perception in all this was and is something not so much seen acutely but perceived—invisible forces setting a compass needle spinning. But I'm also operating under the assumption that my needle is close to calibrated, and that's iffy. To preface: I don't have the answers, but am in a seeking posture, which means I'm working toward them. Though it pragmatically means I often turn out more questions than answers—tough break for me and a few others that might look to me for them, like students.

I see many contemporary-mainstream churches utilizing art that might be communal in scope but can't be easily practiced alone, or even wholeheartedly as a group. Many—maybe most?—people can't sing, paint, or play an instrument. It's good to participate in these things as best you can, but that's almost always felt passive to me. I don't think I'm alone in this.

But language is the most common thread we share, and I think the task of a seeking believer is to be attentive to that language: our words are the best tools we have for writing the narratives or reciting the poems of our lives. You're the only one with your voice, and I'd like to hear the timbre and pitch of that unique song directly, not just as a sound along with other sounds. And I'm less concerned with quality than honesty, though I know not everyone is.

The other issue—which I think is more serious—is that, often in the Church, art is only valuable as a tool for evangelism or expressing the power and grace of God, which is sad to me. Not the *power and grace* bit, but the *only valuable* bit. This kind of uncomplicated-ness frightens me a bit because it lacks honesty and exploration.

It seems to me that collective, contemporary worship practices often leave out some important things that are strewn over the passages of the Bible, like asking tough questions, communal lament, direct address, or earnest doubt—all things a faithful seeker needs. In this way, art is being used *by* the Church rather than *in* the Church, or even better, *as* the Church.

Enter the idea and experiment of Antler (and sacred collisions!)—a teaching and resource platform aiming to help people interested in this intersection of faith and imagination find it, cultivate it, and allow it to change their lives and communities.

I love helping people develop their creative skills and I travel to facilitate on-site workshops or private consultation to people interested in using creative writing or creativity as devotional practices for spiritual formation. I love teaching people to dive into their natural talents with language and asking questions about our spiritual nature—giving them permission to allow their faith and imagination to collide.

Along those same lines what was your "sacred collision between faith and imagination?" Why place creative writing at the center of your new organization?

Thinking about, writing about, and trying to understand the Incarnation has been a sacred collision for me. I wonder what the implications of such a provocative claim should be to me on a daily basis—somehow 'don't sin so much' seems crass and vague. I don't think the Incarnation is about resisting, but about adding to, making new. I also don't think it's tough to see that Incarnation is ultimately an act of divine creativity—God revised in a concrete way.

I wonder how seriously I can take the Incarnation if I'm not willing to allow creative practice to shape my own life. So I go about the activities of my day after I've spent a bit of the morning in focused time of writing—making my words onto the flesh of paper. The more I practice, the more I see the world alive. And that vision gives me a joyful shiver. Because I'm in the world, I can make things come into the world out of the fragments of me I'm trying to understand. We can add to the world by creating—make it richer, bring together all the pieces. We can all do it. Creativity isn't a gift for a select few, but for all of us.

I wanted to create a platform that marries my interests, skills, and potential with the same qualities I believe all people have within. I've taught in a variety of settings and have had students of all walks of life and age. And I've noticed a trend: the practice of writing changes people. Engaging in creating something—even something very simple or small—marks a shift and ushers in a new paradigm.

How do these creative endeavors deepen contemplative efforts and "flesh out" faith?

Perspectives always evolve. I started to see a real need for a fleshing out of faith as I had children, I think. So many things about your world change when kids enter it. I started to see how much my kids—who are just eleven months apart—desired intentionality, not just attention. Maybe that's a good definition of what poetry is to me in some ways—a moving toward intentionality via attention.

In my daily writing—often while the kiddos are sitting at the table with me doodling in their journals—I started to see there was a time in my life (when I was a child) where there were no accidents, or maybe better said, where every accident opened to something new; where every accident could make something very real and very beautiful, only by the fact that it existed and I had made it. My kids have shown me that the business of being child-like is making the loveliest mess you can make. And I think that same principle applies to creating.

In my own faith, I think I'm starting to see that God doesn't come to do something as inconsequential as fix the little messes we've made—God comes to shepherd that mess into something complete, which is different than perfection, or even wholeness. And there's more to the Christ story than just "getting saved," though redemption is a huge part of the narrative. But if we leave it at that, we're utilitarian to a fault, childishly self-centered, and blindly simplistic. For me, the get-saved scenario allows too much room for neglect of the world that "God so loves" and often lacks the compassionate intention I feel I'm called to cultivate from the everyday.

What does that say about creative practice as a whole for you?

God coming into the world has implications of revision that move beyond our individualized experience and affect our lives together in community—people should 'get saved' so the human community might be affected by faith, hope, and charity, not so that they can simply join Christianity and enjoy some perks. God is in the serious business of revision by helping us to re-vision the world toward something complete. To paraphrase a saint—God won't change the world without us.

For me, poetry is the best way to awaken to the divinity that's both inside and around us and to prepare my spirit to bring God's Word into the world—not in an imperialistic or combative fashion, but by way of seeking peace.

I guess—and I know there's been lots of clamor about this lately—the upshot is that I'm just not certain that we have to wait for Heaven, that it can't be quietly trumpeted into this world, into this moment, beginning with our everyday actions. I want a faith that isn't just about the future, or the after-life, but also about the present, and the now-life. And even if Heaven can't be brought here and is in the future, I feel called to make the most of what God has made in this world—to use my gifts to make peace here—not the ever-distant next one. "The Kingdom of God is at-hand" might just be a reference to holding a pen.

What is your challenge to those communities who have not yet started exploring the intersection of faith and imagination? How do you encourage people for whom this is unfamiliar ground?

I've adopted the practice of writing every day—a practice held by many people I know and respect, and many of my favorite writers. All people should do that, I think—how much more interesting the world would be, and peaceful?

I write about anything and everything—nothing gets left out, no matter how strange it seems. Geez, if you could see my journals . . . Almost every one of my little entries is 98%

ephemeral junk and 2% interesting or remotely usable—not great percentages. Yours will be the same—it doesn't matter; do it any way. And do it every day. And do it for at least twenty to thirty minutes.

Often I hear people say that they're unsure of their abilities or don't know where to begin. If that's the case then you should adjust your expectations and know that you're not expected to do too much—that's some of the most freeing advice you'll ever hear, I think. What you write each day doesn't have to look or be "good," it just has to be you—true to who and what you're trying to be. True to the creation that you are, and the new creation you're becoming.

Need ideas? Here are some things you could do during your devotional time with a nothing-to-lose mentality—pick a new one every morning: "journal"; describe what's directly in front of you or out the window; describe anything near you using all five senses; make and tinker with a poem; rewrite something you wrote the day before, add and subtract; write down a memory from childhood, a family story, or a dream you've had; account for your experience over the past twenty-four hours; write down and answer questions you've been thinking about; write in the voice of someone else you know or have known and give yourself advice; go outside and sit in the same place several days in a row and write down the things you see—how does the world look different?; reflect and pray, be specific; write reflections on what you're reading, listening to, or studying; write down something you overheard and give it a back-story; rewrite poems, quotes, or anything that strikes, irritates, or astonishes you. That should give you a good head start. Contact me via thisisantler.com if you want more to do or have questions!

Next, get with others in your faith community on Sunday morning and try something different. Instead of the traditional Sunday School lesson, come together for a workshop—read aloud and discuss what you've written in the previous week. How are you starting to see a small change in your spiritual life from these intentional creative practices; how can your practices as a Christian influence your writing, your creativity? Heck, get together after your church service and use the verses from the service as a springboard for creative and reflective writing. Sit down and write for twenty minutes then share what you've written on the spot—no vacillating. Do creative writing exercises together. Make together. Nothing binds a community together like making something and sharing it. Again, if you want specific ideas, don't hesitate to contact me.

Most of all, remember that writing is quiet, intentional, and patient work. But it's work where nothing is ever wasted. Everything you put down has some value, something to offer—everything gives some small redemption. Even if it just proclaims a way into the next moment of awakening. ᴄᴈ

your voice here.

Through onsite workshops, print media, and digital content, Antler exists to help people engage creativity as a devotional practice for spiritual formation. Now that you've finished *Making Manifest*, take the next step and join the conversation going on all over the web! Go back through your book and send us some of the work you've done that seems awakened, crying out for other readers, a reaching forward from your pages!

Visit **thisisantler.com** for up-to-date articles, resources, and community building tools and post some of your writing from *Making Manifest* to our Facebook page! If you'd like to set up a free video chat session with Dave to discuss what you're doing in your faith community, contact him via the Antler website.

Like us on Facebook (facebook.com/thisisantler), and follow us on Twitter (@thisisantler; @daveharrity) or Instagram (@daveharrity). Let us know you're out there scribbling!

thisisantler.com